# FROM INFINITY
# TO MAN

# EDUARD SHYFRIN

# FROM INFINITY
# TO MAN

THE FUNDAMENTAL IDEAS OF KABBALAH
WITHIN THE FRAMEWORK OF INFORMATION THEORY AND
QUANTUM PHYSICS

First published in 2019 by White Raven Publishing

ISBN 978-1-911195-84-9

Also available as an ebook
ISBN 978-1-911195-85-6

Typeset by Jill Sawyer Phypers
Cover design by Alice Moore

Dedicated to my parents,
Vladimir Shyfrin and Eugeniya Aleksandrovskaya

# ACKNOWLEDGEMENTS

I would like to express my gratitude to the Chief Rabbi of Russia, Berel Lazar, to the President of the Federation of Jewish Communities of Russia, Aleksandr Boroda, and to all of my family members. Also, a special thank you to Yanki Tauber, for his editorial support.

# CONTENTS

For those who would like to understand the mysteries of Creation.

*From Infinity to Man*, by Eduard Shyfrin PhD, businessman and philanthropist, discusses the creation of worlds as described in Kabbalah, as well as the problem of evil and the purpose of the human soul from the point of view of modern information theory and both classical and quantum physics. The author shows how the main views of Kabbalah correspond to the scientific approach to creation.

*From Infinity to Man* is an invitation to consider the puzzle of the world's origin and our place in it, and will be of interest to any thinking reader.

# FOREWORD

Mr Eduard Shyfrin is a most unique person. In addition to many other successful endeavours, he has dedicated himself for decades to the study of physics and other sciences. Throughout the last decade he has pursued the study of Torah literature, across its enormous spectrum, with an unquench-able thirst and with enormous tenacity and fortitude. Eduard has most particularly been drawn to the esoteric dimension of the Kabbalah and the fountains of Chasidic mysticism with a desire to penetrate the depths of Torah wisdom to the maximum extent of his ability. He studies diligently and assiduously and exhibits a rare passion for the deepest divine secrets that are embedded in nature and revealed in the Torah and particularly in the Kabbalah.

Thus Eduard is no ordinary physicist. For him the study of science is not only a scholarly pursuit; it is also a religious enterprise. In contradistinction to so many others, Eduard does not see any contradiction between Torah and Science. On the contrary, his experience has been that the more he learns, the more he discovers harmony and congruence between the Torah and the field of scientific enquiry. His understanding of physics and his reading of Torah have enabled him to confirm more than ever before that the G-d of Nature and the G-d of Revelation is truly One. He seeks to discover parallel patterns in Torah and Science and endeavours to find harmonious trends in the respective disciplines. His enthusiasm for this enterprise has moved him to articulate his thoughts in writing and share his ideas with others.

Thus the volume *From Infinity to Man* is not merely another book; it is a tomb that gives testimony to deep religious quest and arduous investigation; a labour of love! It is a volume that calls for other students of the divine and *le-havdil* the mundane to join the pursuit for the truth that originates in the ultimate blueprint of the divine Architect and permeates through the entirety of the universe He has created.

Mr Eduard Shyfrin is an exemplary model for the Jewish People in yet another way. He is a business man and a philanthropist of high standing. His multifaceted activities demand that he travel and invest substantial time and effort in pursuits other than learning. Yet he has found the time and energy to study Torah with great intrigue and ever-increasing love. He has illustrated that when there is a true will to engage in the study of Torah it is possible for the most busy and preoccupied professional and activist to find the time space to connect to G-d Almighty through the study of His Torah.

I believe that *From Infinity To Man* will be received with intrigue and will generate much enthusiasm for learning. I propose that Eduard Shyfrin's search for synthesis between Torah and Science will inspire others to follow his example. I am confident that Eduard himself will reap much benefit from his tireless efforts in studying and probing the depths of the Torah, and his ever-increasing commitment to Torah values and practices will yield continued blessing and success for Am Yisrael.

Chaim Rapoport, London, England
Rosh Chodesh Kislev 5779

# PREFACE

We know that Hasidism is both a philosophical teaching and a way of life. As a way of life, it is always on view: a Hasid is easily recognisable by the way he prays and in his happiness at serving God, so it is with good reason that, in literature and art, Hasidim are often portrayed dancing. However, the essence of Hasidism as a religious and philosophical teaching, and its particular contribution to the Jewish spiritual tradition, is much more difficult to define.

In fact, the principles of faith in God and knowledge of God were formed long before Hasidism. The medieval Jewish scholar Maimonides (also known by the acronym Rambam) writes: 'The foundation of all foundations and the pillar of wisdom is to know that there is a Primary Being who brought into being all existence.' The whole of Kabbalah is dedicated to setting down knowledge about God and the higher worlds.

With regard to Hasidism's special contribution to the sphere of theoretical philosophy, the main concept that Hasidic teaching has given to Judaism is the significantly deeper awareness of the principle of the oneness of God. As the Mitteler Rebbe – son of the Alter Rebbe, who in 1775 founded the Hasidic movement Chabad – writes in his preface to the book *Imrei Binah*: 'I know, having heard from my father in his teachings, his public speaking, and in private conversations, that the idea of Hasidism is to give people an understanding of the nature of the oneness of God. This must be understood through reason and felt by the heart – according to each person's capabilities.'

Strictly speaking, the particular essence of Hasidic service to God is a direct consequence of Hasidism as a philosophical teaching. Hasidic teaching explains the relationship between man and God, and provides an understanding of who God is for us, and how He interacts with us. The more deeply we understand this, the more this understanding influences our daily lives – it explains to us how to serve God, how to love God, how to pray, and how to be happy in our service.

How does Hasidism explain the principle of the oneness of God, *ahdut ha-Shem*? The main idea is not simply that God is one. It is not even just that God is everywhere. The main concept is that God is EVERYTHING. There is nothing except God! The Baal Shem Tov, the 18th-century founder of Hasidism, formulated this principle: 'Everything is God, and God is everything.' Therefore, the whole world, which was created by God, exists within God. As the Alter Rebbe wrote: 'The whole world is like a small ray inside the sun.' God creates this world anew every second. The Divine is the life energy of everything that exists in the world. In other words, the world is not an independent entity, but solely a manifestation of Divine energy.

It is interesting to note that only within the lifetime of our generation has physics established that matter is the realisation of energy, while the founder of Hasidism realised this from studying the Torah two and a half centuries ago!

We know that the Divine in the world is hidden. That is why it can seem to humanity that the world is something separate from God. However, we also know that God created mankind and entrusted him with the mission of revealing the Divine in the world. Consequently, mankind has, by definition, the opportunity to make such a discovery: he cannot rightly claim that he is unable to fulfil the mission because he is too limited or his life is too short. Since God is everything, that means that not only does He know everything, but he also governs everything – anywhere and everywhere! When a person fulfils the will of God, he should not and cannot have doubts about whether or not he will succeed. God watches over everything: if it is the will of God, then a person cannot fail.

In exactly the same way, a person has no right to say that he is not in a position to discover the Divine because the world has put obstacles in his way. The world is also God, and everything in the world is God: food and drink, money, time and everything else. All aspects of our lives – work and rest, knowledge and creativity, science and technology – everything is inseparably connected with God, and everything is interconnected through God! Therefore, all of this can and should be used in order to fulfil the mission of mankind.

There is another conclusion, which is no less important. There is no need to worry about scientific ideas, or fear that science will suddenly 'prove that there are errors in the Torah'. Science is also a part of God, and it can and should help us to reveal the Divine in the world. In this context, Hasidism not only refrains from contradicting science, but, as a result, it steers mankind towards increasing his knowledge and developing his scientific potential. Hasidism stems from the concept that believing in God is essential, but not sufficient: we must also strive to know and understand! What is Chabad? It is *Chochma-Binah-Daat* – 'Wisdom-Understanding-Knowledge'!

This is the principal idea in the book you are now holding in your hands. The research of Eduard Shyfrin, a long-standing active member of our community and my great friend, provides convincing answers to many of the questions that trouble people in our age of rapid developments in science and technology. The author analyses the wisdom of the Torah through the prism of modern science, and examines the achievements of scientific progress through the prism of the Torah. Then it emerges quite logically and harmoniously that the views of the Torah determine the path of human progress, while the most recent discoveries find their confirmation in the words of the Lord.

In addition, Mr Shyfrin himself is a living embodiment of the theory that everything in the world is interconnected. He is a successful businessman while at the same time avidly studying the Torah, and he is a professional scientist as well as conscientiously observing the commandments. Everything in him is in harmony – one thing organically complements another, and everything comes together to help him reach a new, higher level of the material and spiritual, and to move closer to God.

I am certain that, after reading this book, you will see the thinking of our sages in a new way, as expressed in the treatise *Pirkei avot* (5:26): 'Delve into it [the Torah], and continue to delve into it for everything is in it, and through it you will understand everything … and never part from it, for you will find no better portion than it.'

Chief Rabbi of Russia
Berel Lazar

# INTRODUCTION

## WHY RELIGION AND SCIENCE?

The relationship between religion and science has troubled humanity's greatest thinkers since the creation of religion and science. The objective of religion is to lead a person to the realisation that God is the Creator of everything, to impart knowledge of the laws of Creation, to establish a framework for the interaction of mankind with God, and to illuminate a person's role and objectives in life.

The objective of science is to discover, and gain knowledge of, the natural laws endowed by God to all of Creation. Science expresses until-then hidden connections between natural phenomena in the non-mysterious and logical language of mathematics, thus expanding our understanding of the natural world. Science is very adept at explaining how things work, but struggles when confronted with the question of why they work like that. More than that, science does not give us answers for some fundamental questions: Why are we here? What is the meaning of life? How should we live? To name just a few.

On the other hand, the Torah is not a textbook of physics or mathematics. We should not look for equations or formulae within it. Torah is the wisdom of the Creator given to us as infomation. This information (Torah) radically and forever changed the course of humanity. The Torah is the only book in the world whose author is forever living. By learning the Torah, we learn about the fundamental nature of Creation and about our role and objective in Creation.

The relationship between religion and science has in our time become more important than ever. There are several reasons for this. First, science was for centuries the realm of the lonely scholar, and was denied to the public, conducted behind the closed doors of universities, with little impact on the life of the ordinary man. Today, the opposite is true – science has become accessible to the public, and influences the everyday life of every man, woman and child on the planet. Second, before the advent of the 20th century, science was limited to describing the world in classical terms. The discoveries of quantum physics and special and general relativity opened wholly new facets of reality for us. We cannot intuitively understand how a particle can be in two places at once, nor can we wrap our heads around the idea that time is not absolute, but in fact flows differently for different observers. All of this requires explanation.

The relationship between religion and science is a two-way street. However, when speaking about science, we have to remember that scientific truths are relative – the theory that seems right to us today could tomorrow be proven wrong, or to be just a small part of a more encompassing theory. Scientific knowledge is based on axioms and postulates; however, even they can change. A good example would be the fifth postulate of Euclidean geometry, which states that parallel lines never cross. In the 19th century, mathematicians decided to see how geometry would change if the fifth postulate were to be disregarded. As a result of that, we discovered Riemannian geometry, which at the time seemed like a mathematical abstraction. Fast-forward several decades, and it transpires that Riemannian geometry perfectly describes the space-time of Einstein's general relativity.

WHY IS KNOWLEDGE NECESSARY?

In the *Zohar*, there is a commentary on a verse from *Bereishit*: 'In the six hundredth year of Noah's life … on this day, all the springs of the great deep were split, and the windows of the heavens opened up' (*Bereishit,* 7:11). In the *Zohar*, this is interpreted thus: 'In the sixth century of the sixth millennium, the gates of supernal wisdom will be opened, as will the springs of earthly wisdom' [2].[1] In turn, the seventh Lubavitcher Rebbe[2] explains this verse from the Torah thus: 'The source of earthly wisdom is our scientific knowledge. By means of this second revolution, or the combining of scientific knowledge and Divine wisdom, the Messianic Era will become closer.'[3]

Therefore, it is only with a combination of faith and knowledge that we will be able to complete Creation and make our world a home for God.

Let us take a look at what our sages have written about knowledge. In the

---

1 Figures in brackets indicate a book listed in the bibliography on page 121.

2 The seventh Lubavitcher Rebbe, Menachem Mendel Schneerson (1902–1994) – the last Rabbi of the Chabad Hasidic movement, an eminent spiritual leader, and a thinker of the modern era.

3 The Mashiach, or Messiah, is the ideal Jewish king, a descendant of King David, who will be sent by God for the salvation of the people of Israel. Waiting for the Mashiach is the 12th of the 13 principles of faith formulated by Rambam. He says: 'I believe with perfect faith in the coming of the Mashiach, and though he may tarry, still I await him every day.'

*Tehillim*, it says: 'The Lord in Heaven looked down upon the sons of men to see whether there is a man of **understanding**, who seeks the Lord' (*Tehillim*, 14:2). It also says: 'O Lord, let me know Your ways; teach me Your paths' (*Tehillim*, 25:4).

In *Kohelet*[4] it says: 'And I applied my heart to enquire and to search with wisdom all that was done under the heaven. It is a sore task that God has given to the sons of men with which to occupy themselves' (*Kohelet* 1:13). It also says: 'The wise man has eyes in its beginning, but the fool goes in the darkness...' (*Kohelet*, 2:14). Commenting on these verses, Ibn Ezra writes: 'A wise man can clearly see the way towards even a distant destination, and proceeds along the straightest path, while a foolish man becomes lost in the darkness and walks in an unknown direction, because the wise man perceives reality through his intellect: his vision is broad-ranging. At the same time, the foolish man's vision is narrow and restricted.' In my opinion, the essence of the *Kohelet's* meaning is that, although wisdom and knowledge 'increase sorrow', only a wise man is capable of helping people to overcome their doubts, correct their shortcomings and find the right path in life.

The prophet Yeshayahu (Isaiah) said: 'The land shall be full of knowledge of the Lord as water covers the sea' (*Yeshayahu*, 11:9).

The prophet Yirmiyahu (Jeremiah) said: 'Thus says the Lord: "Let not the wise man boast of his wisdom, nor the strong man boast of his strength, nor the rich man boast of his riches. But let him that boasts exult in this, that he understands and knows Me"' (*Yirmiyahu*, 9:22–23).

In his philosophical work *The Book of Beliefs and Opinions*, Saadia Gaon[5] asks the question: 'Why did the Almighty create mankind, instilling doubts and uncertainty in him?' He then answers this question: 'This quality was given to mankind according to the plan of Creation, but, with the help of his intellect, mankind will, in time, purify his own knowledge until doubt and uncertainty have been dispelled.' Later, Saadia Gaon writes: 'With the help of knowledge, mankind can improve his inner state and behaviour, and relationships with other people will improve. They will turn towards

---

4 *Kohelet* is one of the most well-known books of the Tanakh. It was written by King Shlomo (Solomon). Its Greek name is Ecclesiastes. The book contains 12 chapters and 222 verses.

5 Saadia Gaon (882–942) – the most eminent Torah scholar of the Gaonim period, and head of the largest Jewish academy in the city of Sura (Babylon) – an important centre for Torah study at the time. He was the author of commentaries on the written text and oral tradition of the Torah. Saadia Gaon's book *The Book of Beliefs and Opinions* is one of the most important and popular works of Jewish philosophy today.

wisdom. This will all become possible when doubt and uncertainty are overcome. Then the knowledge of God will spread everywhere.'

In the same book, Saadia Gaon explains: 'Sometimes our understanding
of the reality which we observe can only become possible with the help of
science, as this confirms reality for us. While studying the world around us,
we must engage with many sciences…' [23].

In *The Guide for the Perplexed*[6] Maimonides[7] comments on an extract
from the Torah, in which Moses is speaking to the Almighty: 'Lord let me
know Your ways … so that I may find favour in Your eyes' (*Shemot*, 33:13),
and concludes that nearness to God and finding favour in the eyes of God
is determined first and foremost by how well a person knows and understands the Almighty. In the second volume of *The Guide for the Perplexed*,
Maimonides writes this allegory: 'Let us imagine a city, in the centre of
which there is a palace surrounded by a wall. A ruler lives in the palace. The
townspeople want to reach him. However, they cannot all find the wall:
only a few manage to reach it, some find their way into the inner courtyard,
and only the chosen are able to enter the palace.' According to Maimonides,
people who do not possess knowledge are unable to even find the wall.

In this book, while examining one of the most important questions of
Judaism on the subject of how the Almighty leads the world, Maimonides
states that God watches more closely a person with a developed intellect and
with a similarly high level of knowledge of the Torah.

When discussing the concept of love for the Almighty, which is most
important in Judaism, Maimonides states that the essence of love for God
lies in the desire to understand and recognise Him [7].

### HOW CAN WE ACQUIRE KNOWLEDGE?

It was mentioned above that the Almighty gave us a tool for acquiring
knowledge – intellect. In *The Guide for the Perplexed*, in a commentary on a
phrase from the Torah about how we are created in the image and likeness of
God, Maimonides writes that the main way in which we are like God is the

---

6  Maimonides' philosophical work *The Guide for the Perplexed*, written in Arabic using the Hebrew
alphabet during the 12th century, is his most important work of philosphy. It is aimed primarily at
intellectuals who measure their faith against the yardsticks of science and philosophy. *(Henceforth,
all notes are by the editor, unless otherwise stated.)*

7  Maimonides (Rambam or Moses ben Maimon; 1135–1204) – an eminent Jewish philosopher,
Torah expert and doctor, who was the greatest representative of the brilliant host of medieval
thinkers in the golden age of Spanish Jewish culture.

fact that we have an intellect. He explains that the very first human had an intellect, with the help of which he was able to correctly name the animals. This explanation can be expanded. In his commentary on the first chapter of *Bereishit*, Nachmanides[8] writes: 'After the creation of the primary matter, the Almighty created nothing more. He only formed and made, since, from this, he brought all things into existence, then clothed them in different forms and transformed them.' With the help of intellect, mankind, too, can give matter new forms and transform them.

Maimonides and Ibn Ezra[9] wrote that it is the intellect that connects a person with the Almighty. By developing his intellectual capabilities, a person strengthens his connection with the Almighty and vice versa.

We are all given different intellectual potential. In the *Tanya*, the Alter Rebbe, Shneur Zalman of Liadi,[10] writes: 'Wisdom and understanding are a gift from the Almighty' [8]. No one knows whether our intellectual potential is limited. In my opinion it is. Not everyone can become Einsteins or great Torah scholars. **But this does not mean that a person has the right to refrain from intellectual development. We must follow that path, and the Almighty will decide how far we will reach.**

The clearest confirmation of the above is to be found in the story of Rabbi Akiva (AD 50–137). Until the age of forty, he was an illiterate shepherd and, apparently, believed his intellectual capacity to be very limited. One day, however, seeing how drops of water wore away a stone, he decided to study and become a great Torah scholar. His potential for intellectual development turned out to be huge.

## JUDAISM AND SCIENCE

During the process of their development, the paths of Judaism and science have converged and diverged. Over the course of almost two thousand years, the only dominant scientific theories in the civilised world were the

---

8  Rabbi Moses ben Nachman (Ramban; c.1195–1270) – one of the preeminent sages of Spanish Jewry, Nachmanides authored many important works of biblical commentary, Torah law and Jewish mysticism. Towards the end of his life, he made aliyah to Israel and revived the Jewish community in Jerusalem.

9  Rabbi Abraham Ibn Ezra (c.1092–1167) – a philosopher, *Tanakh* commentator, poet and doctor. He was the author of scientific works on astronomy and mathematics. Spain.

10  Rabbi Shneur Zalman of Liadi (the Alter Rebbe; 1745–1812) – founder of the Hasidic movement, Chabad, Kabbalist, and author of the *Tanya*, the main book of Hasidism.

philosophies of Plato and Aristotle, the geometry of Euclid, the Ptolemaic system, and astrology. Attempts to combine Judaism and philosophy, and to present Judaism as a faith founded on rational thought, were first made by the Babylonian Gaonim, the most prominent representative of whom was Saadia Gaon. In *The Book of Beliefs and Opinions*, he proposes the principle of rational thought, and a philosophical and scientific approach with the aim of attaining knowledge of God.

With the decline of Jewish centres of learning in Babylonia, the rationalist tradition was brilliantly continued by Spanish Jews such as Judah Halevi,[11] Maimonides, Nachmanides and Ibn Ezra. The Spanish Torah scholars possessed the highest level of scientific knowledge available at that time. This is excellently demonstrated in Maimonides' great work, *The Guide for the Perplexed*, in which the laws of the Creator are explained and commented upon both from the position of the Torah and from the point of view of Greek and Arabic philosophy.

Unfortunately, following the expulsion of Jews in Spain, the paths of Judaism and science diverged. In the centuries following the expulsion, mysticism prevailed in Judaism. Many people saw mysticism as opposing rationalism. In my view, this is wrong. They are both inseparable parts of Judaism, and ultimately complementary to each other. The teaching of the Arizal[12] on *tzimtzum*,[13] for example, coincides in many ways with modern notions of the creation of the world.

Jewish mysticism was born together with Judaism. By its definition, something mystical is irrational and unscientific. The problem, in my opinion, is that the ideas of Jewish mysticism were many centuries ahead of their time, and only now can we see that they are in fact supportive of science. It is this theme that we will explore in this book.

---

11 Judah Halevi (c.1075–1141) – a philosopher and poet. Spain.

12 Arizal (Rabbi Isaac ben Solomon Luria Ashkenazi, or the Ari; 1534–1572) – the greatest of venerable men, miracle worker and expert on the mysteries of the Torah. He was the founder of a new Kabbalah movement known as Lurianic Kabbalah.

13 *Tzimtzum* – a Kabbalist concept, conventionally referring to the process of God's 'contraction' of His infinite self-expression to form an 'empty space', allowing for the existence of the various 'worlds' of Creation.

# A SHORT INTRODUCTION TO KABBALAH

This book does not aim to provide a comprehensive course on Kabbalah (there is already a vast number of works on this subject). In this work, I analyse the Kabbalah from the point of view of the scientific knowledge available to us today. Therefore, listed below in brief are the main points of Kabbalah, as well as a few concepts from information theory and quantum physics, to facilitate navigation through the text.

## A BRIEF HISTORY

Kabbalah is a teaching based on the deep understanding of the multi-layered meaning of the Torah. It describes the creation of worlds by the Almighty, the theory of *sefirot* (Divine attributes), the laws of functionality and the connection of worlds, the creation of humankind, the human soul, and the role and tasks of humanity in Creation.

The Jewish mystical tradition was born with Judaism itself. It assumed a variety of forms but has never stopped. The form of Kabbalah that we know today arose in Provence (Southern France) in the 12th century. Its founders were Rabbi Abraham ben Isaac of Narbonne,[14] his son-in-law Abraham ben David (Raavad)[15] and Isaac the Blind.[16] Kabbalah subsequently became widespread among the Jewish communities in Spain. The most prominent centre for Kabbalah study was formed in Spain in the 13th century. It was known as the Gerona School, after the Catalonian town of Gerona where some eminent Kabbalists lived and studied. Among their number were Judah ben

---

14  Rabbi Abraham ben Isaac of Narbonne (c.1110–1158)– a Torah scholar and Kabbalist. France.

15  Abraham ben David of Posquières (Raavad; 1125–1198) – a pupil of Rabbi Abraham ben Isaac of Narbonne, eminent Torah sage, expert in Jewish law, and head of the Jewish sages of Provence. He is famous for his commentaries on the Babylonian Talmud and Maimonides' Mishnah Torah. France.

16  Isaac the Blind (1160–1235) – a well-known Kabbalist of the Gerona School, and son of Abraham ben David. Many researchers believe that Isaac the Blind was the author of the book called the *Bahir*, the most important work on Kabbalah.

Yakar,[17] Ezra ben Solomon,[18] Azriel,[19] Moses ben Nachman (Nachmanides or Ramban), Abraham ben Isaac Gerondi, and others. In the 13th century, the Spanish Kabbalists included Abraham Abulafia,[20] the founder of 'Prophetic Kabbalah'. At the end of the 13th century, Moses ben Shem-Tov de Léon[21] from Guadalajara published one of the main books of Kabbalah, *Sefer ha'Zohar* ('The Book of Radiance'), ascribed to the *Tannaim*[22] Rabbi Shimon bar Yochai.[23] Another prominent 13th-century Kabbalist was Joseph Gikatilla.[24] In the 14th century, the Kabbalist tradition was continued by Solomon ben Abraham Adret (Rashba),[25] Isaac ben Todros[26] and others.

---

17  Judah ben Yakar – a Torah scholar, and one of the authors of the *Tosafot* – extensive commentaries on the Talmud. France.

18  Ezra ben Solomon – Torah scholar and Kabbalist. Spain.

19  Azriel (1160–1238) – Torah scholar, well-known Jewish Kabbalist of the Gerona School in the 12th century, and pupil of Isaac the Blind. Teacher of Nachmanides.

20  Abraham Abulafia (1240–c.1292) – an eminent Kabbalah scholar. He wrote 22 books on Kabbalah. The most well-known of these are: *Sefer Sitrei Torah* ('Secrets of the Torah'), *Chaye ha-Olam ha-Ba* ('Life in the World to Come') and *Or ha-Sekhel* ('Light of the Intellect'). Rabbi Abulafia continued the new path towards attaining hidden knowledge. He developed 'Prophetic Kabbalah' methods, leading him to achieve the level of prophet.

21  Moses ben Shem-Tov de Léon (1250–1305) – rabbi, Kabbalist, author and transcriber of Kabbalist books, including the *Zohar*. Spain.

22  *Tanna* (Aram. *'teacher'*) – a sage from the time of the compilation of the *Mishnah*. The views of the Tannaim concerning every instance of Jewish law are included in the *Mishnah* and the *Baraita*. The *Gemara* distinguishes between the Torah scholars of two periods – the *Tannaim* and the *Amoraim* (the latter lived at the time of the compilation of the Talmud). The era of the Tannaim began with the pupils of Shammai and Hillel. It lasted approximately two hundred years and included the years of King Herod's rule, the destruction of the Temple, and the *Bar Kokhba* revolt. The era ended during the time of Rabbi Judah ha-Nasi, compiler and redactor of the *Mishnah*, and it was followed by the *Amoraim* era.

23  Rabbi Shimon bar Yochai (Rashbi; 2nd century AD) – one of the most prominent Jewish teachers of the law, a sage of the Torah, *tanna*, a founder of Kabbalah, and author of one of the main Kabbalist books, the *Zohar*.

24  Joseph ben Abraham Gikatilla (1248–1305 or later) – one of the representatives of the Spanish Kabbalah school. One of his most well-known works is *Sha'are Ora* ('Gates of Light').

25  Rabbi Solomon ben Abraham Adret (Rashba; c.1235–1310) – a pupil of Nachmanides, an authoritative sage of the 13th and 14th centuries, and a Jewish law expert. He officially held the post of Chief Rabbi of Barcelona, although he actually acted as chief rabbi of Spain. He wrote a range of commentaries on various Talmudic treatises, and compiled a new code of laws – *Torat ha-Bayit ha-Aruk* ('The Complete Law of the House') – and other books.

26  Isaac ben Todros – Spanish rabbi, Talmud scholar and doctor in the early 14th century.

After the Jews were exiled from Spain in 1492, the Kabbalah centre moved to Safed in the Land of Israel. Among the Safed Kabbalists, most worthy of note were Moses Yaakov Cordovero,[27] Joseph Caro,[28] Arizal and Hayyim Vital.[29] Later, the Kabbalist tradition was successfully continued by Hasidic *tzadikim* in Ukraine and Poland. Of particular interest is the founder of the Habad movement, Rabbi Shneur Zalman of Liadi, also known as Alter Rebbe [20].

The main books of Kabbalah include *Sefer Yetzirah* ('The Book of Formation'), traditionally ascribed to our forefather Abraham, *Sefer HaBahir*, attributed to Rabbi Nehunya ben HaKanah,[30] *Sefer ha'Zohar*, *Pardes Rimonim* by Moses Cordovero, the teachings of Arizal written by his pupil Hayyim Vital, and the works of the Alter Rebbe – the *Tanya*, *Torah Or*, and so on [25].

## THE MAIN CONCEPTS OF KABBALAH

### EIN SOF ('NOT FINITE')

In Kabbalist traditions, the Almighty can be viewed in two states: *Ein Sof* (this refers to God's infinite self-expression), and the Almighty in connection with His creation. The term *Ein Sof* first appeared in the works of Isaac the Blind and Azriel of Gerona. According to Kabbalah, the Almighty is only accessible to our understanding in connection with His creation. We cannot understand the Almighty in the state of *Ein Sof*. We do not find Him referred to in this way in the Torah and the *Tanakh*. In the state of *Ein Sof*, the Almighty is absolutely simple, whole, has no emotions or attributes, and is not subject to change.

In the state of *Ein Sof*, the Creator is manifest as absolute perfection. He

---

27  Rabbi Moses Yaakov Cordovero (Ramak; 1522–1570) – one of the greatest Kabbalists of all time. He founded his own academy in Safed, where Arizal studied. His main work was *Pardes Rimonim* ('Orchard of Pomegranates'). In this work, Ramak summarised and systematised three centuries of Kabbalist ideas, beginning with the publication of the *Zohar*.

28  Rabbi Joseph ben Ephraim Caro (1488–1575) – the greatest law teacher of all generations, the founder of the *Shulchan Aruch* ('Set Table') code and *Beth Yoseph* ('House of Joseph'), a fundamental commentary on Jewish Laws.

29  Rabbi Hayyim bar Joseph Vital (1543–1620) – one of the greatest Kabbalists of all time. A pupil of Arizal and Rabbi Moses Cordovero. He wrote down the knowledge he had been given by Arizal in two large books: *Etz Hayyim* ('Tree of Life') and *Etz Hadaat* ('Tree of Knowledge').

30  Nehunya ben HaKanah – second generation *tanna*. Praised for his piety. His name is often associated with pursuing hidden wisdom.

does not discern between good and evil, or heaven and earth. The epithets usually used in prayers cannot be applied to him ('great', 'mighty', etc.). According to Maimonides, in the state of *Ein Sof* God can only be understood in terms of negatives – for example, 'never-ending' – in view of His infinite nature [7].

In Kabbalah, *Ein Sof* is the root of all roots, which is in keeping with the description of God by some philosophers (Aristotle, Spinoza) who called Him the cause of all causes. Moses Cordovero wrote of the Almighty in the state of *Ein Sof*: 'You should know that you must not use expressions such as "blessed", "praised" and so on, with regard to *Ein Sof,* since He cannot be blessed or praised by others, because, in the state of *Ein Sof,* He is the One who blesses, praises and supports all – from the first (highest) point of emanation to the very lowest point. It is impossible to imagine, postulate, or say anything about Him – there is no justice, no mercy, no wrath, no change, no limits, and no process of any kind of quality whatsoever' [25].

Within the reality of *Ein Sof,* no created being with an awareness of its own self can occur and exist. In order to allow created beings to appear with their own 'self', *Ein Sof* emanated and created a system of worlds based on the ten *sefirot.*

### SEFIROT

In the book *Sefer Yetzirah*, it says that everything was created by means of the twenty-two letters of the Hebrew alphabet and the ten *sefirot*, which were called numbers. It says: 'Ten *sefirot* of nothing. Ten and not nine. Ten and not eleven.' Later, it says: 'The ten *sefirot* out of nothing. They appear like lightning and are without end. His word is in them, they are running and returning. Ten *sefirot* out of nothing. Their end enters into their beginning, and their beginning enters into their end, as a flame proceeds from coal' [4].

In Kabbalah, a *sefirah* is allegorically depicted as a vessel filled with light. The *sefirot* are joined together in a system known as the tree of *sefirot* (Fig. 1). The *sefirot* system is the foundation of all worlds, and the channels for Divine Light.

The first *sefirah, Keter* (the Crown), is the intermediary between *Ein Sof* and the rest of the *sefirot* system. It expresses the desire and will of the Creator.

In the next s*efirah, Chochma* (wisdom), eternal light is revealed in the form of finite and recognisable light in the *sefirot* system. *Chochma* represents the first, most primary element of creation that exists in the potential within Divine thought.

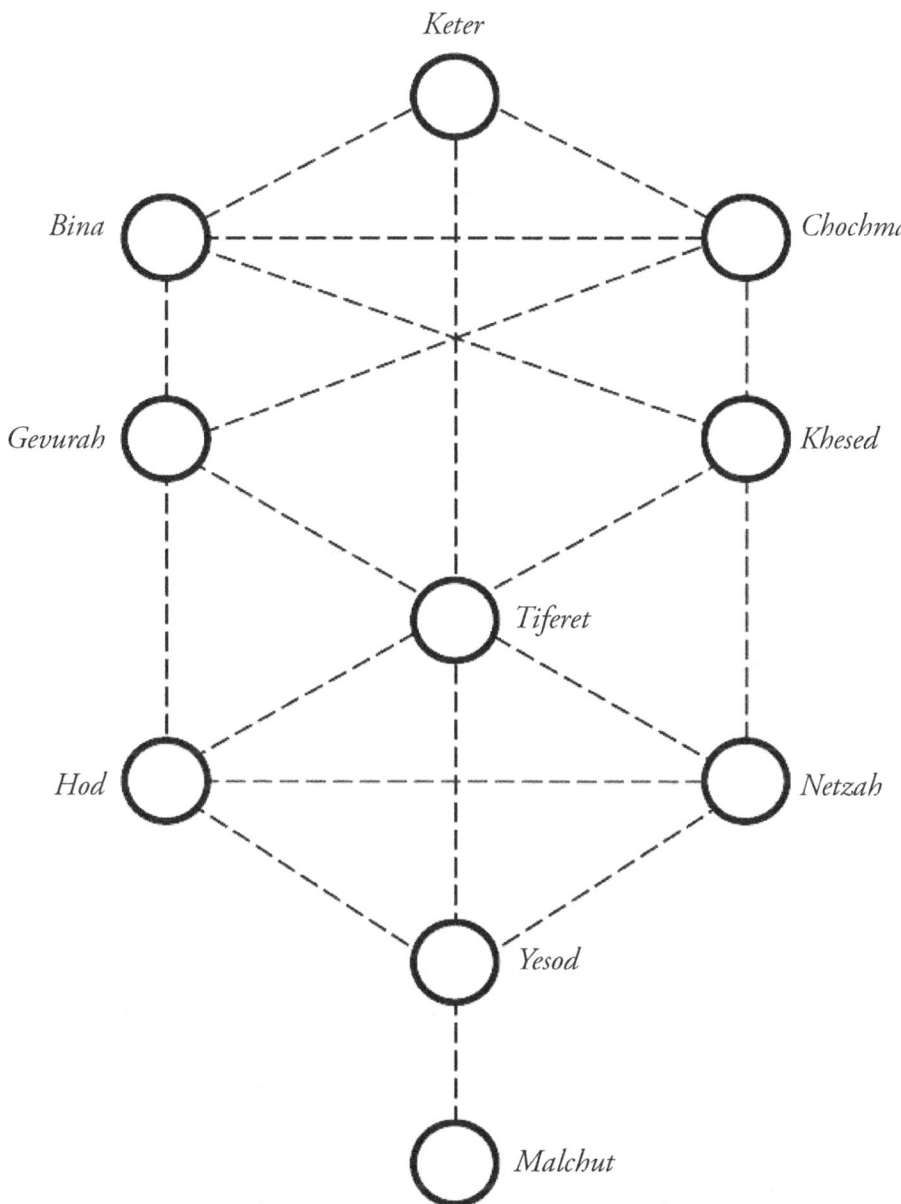

Fig. 1. The tree of *Sefirot*

The third *sefirah*, *Binah* (understanding), represents the realisation of the details inherent in the primordial Divine thought. The attributes of judgement and mercy are woven into the three highest *sefirot*, and only at the level of *Binah* does division occur, although the harmony between the attributes is retained.

The seven lower *sefirot* are divided into six *midot* and the *sefirah* of *Malchut*. The first triad of lower *sefirot* consists of *Chesed*, *Gevurah* and *Tiferet*. *Chesed* (kindness, love, expansion) corresponds to our forefather Abraham. Its characteristics are love, kindness and abundance. *Gevurah* (might, power, judgement, contraction) corresponds to our forefather Isaac. Its characteristics are restraint, brevity and judgement, whereby a person's misdeeds and service are weighed up and a sentence is pronounced. The third *sefirah*, *Tiferet* (beauty), is a harmonising and balancing *sefirah* for *Chesed* and *Gevurah*. It is associated with our forefather Jacob, whose soul combined the characteristics of Abraham and Isaac. At this point, it is important to note the profound idea of the book *Torah Or* concerning the danger of unbalanced character traits. Thus, our forefather Abraham, who possessed *Chesed that was not balanced by Gevurah*, fathered Ishmael, who did not follow the way of his father. Our forefather Isaac, who possessed *Gevurah that was not balanced by Chesed*, fathered Esau, who also did not inherit his tradition. Only Jacob, whose characteristics were all balanced, had sons who all followed his way [9].

The next triad of *sefirot* is *Netzach* (victory), associated with Moses Rabbeinu, *Hod* (splendour), associated with Moses' brother, Aaron the high priest, and *Yesod* (foundation), associated with Joseph, the son of Jacob. The main functions of *Yesod* are the harmonisation of *Netzach* and *Hod*, as well as the transfer of light from the highest *sefirot* to the *sefirah* of *Malchut*. *Malchut* (kingdom) is associated with King David. The light of all *sefirot* systems comes down in the *sefirah* of *Malchut* and, through it, is transferred to lower worlds. The Divine presence in the *sefirah* of *Malchut* is called *Shekhinah*.

According to the teaching of Arizal, apart from the *sefirot* there are also some fundamental principles of the formation of the world, known as *partzufim* (faces). The following *partzufim* are particularly notable: *Abba* (the Father, corresponds with the *sefirah* of *Chochma*), *Imma* (the Mother, corresponds with the *sefirah* of *Binah*), *Arich Anpin* (Long Face, therefore of long-lasting patience), *Atik Yomin* ('Ancient of Days,' which together with *Arich Anpin* corresponds with the *sefirah* of *Keter*), *Zeir Anpin* (literally short-faced, meaning impatient, corresponds with the six *midot* or *qualities*),

*Nukvah d'Zeir* (the female hypostasis of *Zeir*, corresponds with the *sefirah* of *Malchut*). Sometimes *Keter* does not appear, and *Daat* (knowledge) is introduced instead. I will return to the other details of the *sefirot* system, their functional composition and their system of interaction, in later chapters.

## WORLDS

### *Tzimtzum*

I have already mentioned that no created being with an awareness of its own 'self' is possible in *Ein Sof*. According to the teaching of Arizal, the first act of creation was *tzimtzum*. This is the 'contraction' of *Ein Sof* and formation of *tehiru* – the empty space. It contained only the remnants of Divine Light, known as *reshimu*. Compared with the infinite *Ein Sof, tehiru* was like a tiny spot, but it was from this that all levels of existence proceeded. Arizal explains that *tzimtzum* appears as *Gevurah* in the world. According to his teaching, before *tzimtzum* all the powers of the Almighty were in His infiniteness, and they were balanced without any division. However, for the creation of empty space, the Almighty concentrated the roots of *Gevurah*.

Then, into this void, a line of light was directed – *Ohr Ein Sof,* from which worlds later developed. To this day there are many debates about how to understand the process of *tzimtzum* – literally or allegorically. Alter Rebbe rejected the literal understanding. According to his study, *tzimtzum* does not refer to the literal withdrawal of light, but to the reduced ability of the light to reveal itself before transitioning to a hidden state. He writes: 'Therefore *tzimtzum* is called the "occurrence of empty space" or "a place deprived of light", meaning a space where there is an absence of any kind of light, or a discovery that the light has gone away to its source and transitioned to potential existence.' Additionally, Alter Rebbe comments that the concepts of reduction and concealment do not apply to the Almighty Himself, but only to His 'light' (self-expression) [9].

The first reality to emerge after *tzimtzum* was *Adam Kadmon* (primordial man). It contained all the *sefirot* as potential. *Adam Kadmon* is an intermediary realm between *Ein Sof* and the subsequent system of worlds. From the head of *Adam Kadmon* shone forth a light, which took various forms, in particular the outlines of letters and utterances. The light that proceeded from the ears, nose and mouth of *Adam Kadmon* spread out in a straight line and formed the world *Akudim*, in which all the *sefirot* were combined in a single vessel. The light that proceeded from the eyes was divided into separate *sefirot*. Thus, the world of *Nekudim* (spotted world) or the world of *Tohu* (chaos) was formed, where the *sefirot* did not interact with each other.

It is said of the world of *Tohu* that 'Its kings reigned in the land of Edom before the reign of the Children of Israel'. According to Alter Rebbe, the world of *Tohu* is the world of *Gevurah*, which 'possesses enormous power and corresponds to the seven dead kings of Edom. That is why the ten *sefirot* of the world of *Tohu* are called kings' [9]. In this world, a special event took place, which affected the whole structure of creation. Streams of Divine Light emanated into the *sefirot* of the world of *Tohu*. The eight lower *sefirot* were unable to withstand the strong beam of light and shattered into tiny pieces containing sparks of light, while the light itself returned to its source. This event was given the name 'the shattering of the vessels' (*Shevirat ha-Keilim*), and it is difficult to overestimate its importance.

In Kabbalist literature, there are many explanations as to what caused the vessels to shatter. In total, there were 288 sparks of holiness that scattered and 'fell' into our material world. Arizal takes this number from the gematria of the word *merahefet* (hovered) from *Bereishit* 1:2.

The fragments of the broken vessels, according to Arizal's teaching, fell to the lower worlds, breaking into many more, even tinier pieces, and became the seeds of creatures with an awareness of their own 'self'. Impure *kelipot* ('husks') belonging to *sitra achra* – the 'other side', i.e. evil – were formed from these same fragments. Alter Rebbe explains this by saying that the fragments possessed a large sense of their own 'self' and insufficient awareness of Divinity, hence the appearance of evil.

In the example of the world of *Tohu*, the Almighty was convinced that creation cannot exist in such a form, since correction would be impossible in such a world. Creating the opportunity for correction required a fundamental change in the whole configuration of the *sefirot* system, in order to make interaction possible.

### Atzilut, Beriah, Yetzirah and Asiyah

The description of the creation of these worlds is contained in the phrase of the prophet *Yeshayahu*: 'All that is called by My name and for My glory, I created it, I formed it, I also made it' (*Yeshayahu*, 43:7). The words 'All that is called by My name' refer to the world of *Atzilut* (the world of emanation); 'created' refers to the world of *Beriah* (the world of creation); 'formed' refers to the world of *Yetzirah* (the world of formation), and 'made' refers to our material world, *Asiyah* (the world of action). All four worlds contain a system of ten *sefirot*, which interact with each other. Moreover, every *sefirah* contains ten more *sefirot,* and so on, ad infinitum. (We will return to this question in subsequent chapters.) In the world of *Atzilut*, all the vessels of this world are united with the light, and there is no division between them [9]. There, the existence of anything except Divine Light is unthinkable. The lower *sefirah* of the world of *Atzilut, Malchut,* is the *sefirah* of *Keter* for the world of *Beriah*. Archangels, a few souls, and *Gan Eden* (paradise) are already appearing in the world of *Beriah*. The world of *Yetzirah* is populated by angels and souls. The world of *Asiyah* is populated by souls and people.

### LIGHT

The concept of 'Divine Light' is central to Judaism in general, and particularly to Kabbalah. Clearly an analogy between Divine Light and the physical light of our world is, if permissible, extremely limited. The book *Torah Or* contains the following definition: 'The concept of "Divine Light" signifies revelation and proliferation. Because of it, the appearance of the source of the life force of all worlds becomes possible. The very essence of the concept of "light" is connected with revelation and proliferation. Divine Light, unlike the *sefirot* vessels, has no "self". The same can also be said of the light of the Infinite: He Himself is a luminary, and His light is the revelation and proliferation of this luminary, i.e. the Divine life force' [9]. There is a system of classification for the various forms of Divine Light. The light that is called *mimalei* (filling) and *pnimi* (internal) circulates within the system of worlds and *sefirot*. It is able to enter within an entity and be assimilated by it, joining with it from within in order to impart life and vitality to it. This form of light is, by its nature, concealed and limited. The light called *sovev* or *makif* (surrounding or encompassing) is the spiritual light of the Almighty, that is without limits. It cannot be perceived by a single creature. Its influence is unperceivable for Creation, and is the same for all. The infusion of light in a limited, hidden form begins in the *sefirah* of *Chochma* in the world of *Atzilut*. (I will write more about Divine Light in subsequent chapters.) While passing through the chain of worlds, the light takes part in the process of *hishtalshelut* ('evolution' and concealment of light). During this process, as the movement from the highest worlds towards the lowest ones takes place, there is a gradual 'contraction' – the concealment of light. As a result, it reaches our material world in a state of maximum concealment. Every time light passes from a higher level to a lower one, it passes through a *parsa* (a curtain), which is called *hashmal* (from the words for 'to be silent' and 'to speak'). (We will return to this explanation, too, in subsequent chapters.)

The light that descends from higher worlds to lower ones is called 'direct light'. There is also 'returning light', which ascends from below to above. According to the teaching of Arizal, it arises as a result of the collision of direct light with an obstacle at the end of the stages, resulting in a kind of reflection.

## THE OMNISCIENCE OF THE ALMIGHTY

The question of the level of God's omniscience and a person's free will has been the cause of argument and debate in Judaism for many centuries. Alter Rebbe solves this contradiction by dividing the knowledge of the Almighty into two levels: higher and lower knowledge. Higher knowledge (the knowledge of *Ein Sof*), in his words, 'refers to that which He knows and sees, as if making no impact at all'. Higher knowledge corresponds to the light of *sovev*. At the level of higher knowledge, there is no difference between good and evil, as neither reward nor punishment are produced [9]. This is the level of which Maimonides speaks when he says that the Almighty and His knowledge are one [7]. Alter Rebbe writes about this level as follows: 'The level of higher knowledge is the source of forgiveness and mercy, since no flaw or sin can touch this level, which is higher than the vessels of the ten *sefirot*' [9]. The book of *Bamidbar* says: 'He does not look at evil in Jacob, and has seen no perversity in Israel' (*Bamidbar*, 23:21).

Lower knowledge is connected with the vessels and the *midot*, meaning it is in the system of worlds. At this level, reward and punishment takes place. This knowledge corresponds to the light filling the *sefirot* of the worlds of *Atzilut, Beriah, Yetzirah* and *Asiyah*. It can be said that lower knowledge 'works within the regime of real time'. As Alter Rebbe comments, the Almighty does, of course, know everything in advance, but this knowledge is taken to mean higher knowledge, without the mediation of the vessels of the ten *sefirot*, which are called the 'eyes of God wandering around on Earth', by which the Creator views all the events from within time [9].

## NAMES

The Almighty has no name: how can the Giver of names have a name? However, we encounter Him under various names in the Torah. There are quite a lot of them, but we will look at just two – *Havayah* (the tetragrammaton – *yud, hei, vav, hei*) and *Elohim*. These names characterise the various levels of manifestation of the Almighty in relation to the creation of worlds and humanity. The name *Havayah* characterises the attribute of mercy. The letter *yud* corresponds to the *sefirah* of *Chochma*; the first *hei* refers to the *sefirah* of *Binah*; the letter *vav* signifies the six lower *sefirot* (*midot*); and the second *hei* indicates the *sefirah* of *Malchut*.

The name *Elohim* corresponds to the Divine presence in our world, i.e. the *sefirah* of *Malchut*. Its effect is the concealment of Divine Light and a reduction of its intensity. Here, the quality of *Gevurah* is manifest, which corresponds to the name *Elohim*. The gematria of this name relates to the word 'nature' in Hebrew. Alter Rebbe writes: 'After many contractions and concealments, carried out through the name of *Elohim*, Divine Light is clothed in created beings and gives them life, so that they may thus become "something", that is, they will sense the seeming independence of their existence before the Divine "nothing"' [9].

## THE SIN OF ADAM

Before the sin of Adam, all the worlds were a single whole, through which Divine Light circulated freely. The side of evil, *sitra achra,* which occurred as a result of the shattering of the vessels (see 'Worlds', page 14), was completely separated from the side of holiness. Adam was placed in *Gan Eden*, and given the task of 'working and guarding' the garden – that is, to fulfil the commandments – and thus raise the sparks of holiness that had fallen into *sitra achra* back to their source. Therefore, Adam and Eve were present in *Gan Eden* in a state that wasn't fully material (we will discuss this later). Adam possessed a single soul and authority over the world of *Adam Kadmon*.

Several events occurred as a result of Adam's fall. First of all, the unity of the worlds was broken, evil was mixed with good, and consequently, between the zone of *kelipat* (*sitra achra*) and the zone of holiness, a zone of *kelipat nogah* formed, where there is both good and evil. Adam's soul lost its wholeness, and the bodies of Adam and Eve became material. The level of spirituality in the world of *Asiyah* diminished, and its material nature increased. The Divine presence in the world was substantially reduced. This is how the Alter Rebbe describes the process: 'After Adam's fall, it is said: "And the Lord God made for Adam and for his wife shirts of skin, and He dressed them" (*Bereishit,* 3:21), since before the fall, the concealment of light was particularly insignificant. However, after the fall, there was increased opposition; in other words, *kelipat nogah* appeared, which epitomises the clothes of skin' [9]. Alter Rebbe explains the words of the Almighty that follow this action: 'Adam has become like one of us, having the ability of knowing good and evil' (*Bereishit,* 3:22). He writes that these words are addressed to the angels. Hence, the beings in higher worlds know the nature of good and evil. There, though, good and evil are not mixed together, but are separate [9]. If, after tasting the fruit of the tree of life, Adam had remained in *Gan Eden,* then evil would have been given the right to exist for eternity, which would have contradicted the intentions of the Almighty. This was the reason Adam and Eve were banished from *Gan Eden* after the fall.

**THE SOUL**

The soul is a created essence that gives life to all creation. According to the accepted classification in Judaism, a person's soul is divided into several parts: *nefesh* (the vitalising soul), *ruach* (corresponds to the spirit and emotions), *neshama* (the intellectual part of the soul), *chaya* (the highest level of cognitive ability) and *yechida* (a spark of God – the highest level of the soul). Each part of the soul has its own root in higher worlds. *Nefesh* corresponds to the *sefirah* of *Malchut, ruach* to *Zeir Anpin* (the six lower *sefirot*), *neshama* to the *sefirah* of *Binah, chaya* to the *sefirah* of *Chochma,* and *yechida* to the *sefirah* of *Keter.* From my point of view, the most comprehensive 'theory of the soul' is the one developed by Alter Rebbe in the *Tanya* ('The Book of the Intermediates'), *Torah Or* and others. It highlights the three component parts of the soul: Divine, animal and intellectual. Until its descent into the world, the Divine soul was part of the world of *Atzilut.* The purpose of its descending into lower worlds and being clothed in the animal soul of a human is to correct and raise up the animal soul. 'Nevertheless, this descent of the soul is carried out for the sake of its subsequent ascent, since only by coming down is the soul able to study the Torah and fulfil the commandments' [9]. The Divine soul never sins, although its love for the Almighty is constrained and limited by its investment within the animal soul and the body.

All the intentions and actions of the animal soul are directed at our material world. It is 'strong' – its root is in the world of *Tohu,* the predecessor of *Atzilut.* Here, one of the main principles of Kabbalah is realised: 'The lower the level where a created entity is located, the higher its spiritual root.'

Let us examine the structure of the soul, as presented by Alter Rebbe. According to his theory, the soul is 'the whole and indivisible light, which cannot be divided into intellect and *midot*'. The latter serve merely as the 'garments of the soul': in other words, they belong to the soul but do not relate to its essence. Thus, the soul is a whole light whose garments consist of the ten *sefirot*. The structure of the soul corresponds to the structure of the higher spiritual worlds. Hence the words from *Bereishit* 1:26 about how man was created 'in the image and likeness' of the Almighty.

There are a great many combinations of the ten *sefirot* that could occur, and which are like the DNA of a human soul. Which of the components of the human soul is given advantage depends on the correlation of the *sefirot* and the predominance of some trait or aspect over the others. On this topic, Alter Rebbe writes: 'Intellect and emotion are "tools" that the soul uses, just as a woodcutter uses an axe. However, this does not all apply to the essence of a soul that has not been subject to any changes. ... Intellect and *midot* (*sefirot*) are nothing more than powers of the soul, which are reflected in the body but do not capture the essence of the soul' [9].

Where does the soul dwell? From my point of view, this question is incorrect, since the soul has no dimensions in time and space. The founder of Hasidism, Rabbi Israel Baal Shem Tov, emphasised that talking about the dwelling of the soul is wrong: instead, we should speak about where the soul's revelation takes place. Both the animal and the Divine souls are clothed in *sefirot*. The six lower *sefirot* of the Divine soul (*midot*) are called *yetzer ha-tov* (positive impulse). The six lower *sefirot* of the animal soul are called *yetzer ha-ra* (negative impulse). There is a constant struggle between them. The task of the Divine soul is to turn the animal soul towards the Almighty, and towards studying the Torah and fulfilling the commandments. Because the animal soul is so strong, when its passions are redirected towards God, its love for the Almighty can have no limits. The third component part of the human soul – the intelligent soul – is, from the point of view of Alter Rebbe, an 'intermediary' between the Divine and the animal souls, and the means by which the Divine soul can influence the animal soul.

### LETTERS

In the book *Sefer Yetzirah*, it says that the Almighty created everything by means of the twenty-two letters of the Hebrew alphabet and the ten *sefirot*, known as numbers. Alter Rebbe writes: 'The spiritual root of the letters is the *sefirah* of *Keter*, which is higher than *Chochma* and intellect. However, it is first revealed in *Chochma*, since it is impossible to recognise and understand a thing or a thought without the help of letters. The Torah, too, is clothed in letters, although the spiritual root of the letters of the Torah is incomparably higher than the Torah itself, since it is said of the Torah: "The Torah proceeds from *Chochma*", while the root of the letters themselves is considerably higher – in the *sefirah* of *Keter*. The letters signify the attraction of influence from the highest level, whence the Torah appears' [10]. Let us also note the fact that all worlds were created by the utterances of the Almighty, which are also made up of letters.

## THE ROLE OF MANKIND IN CREATION

According to the teaching of Arizal, the role of mankind is to implement the process of *tikun* (correcting the consequences of the shattering of the vessels and the sin of Adam) and attract Divine Light into the world. By means of Torah study, prayer, and fulfilling the commandments, a person must raise the sparks of holiness, which have fallen into the realm of *sitra achra*, back up to the higher worlds, turning darkness into light and thus destroying evil. It is worth noting that the commandments have their spiritual root in the *sefirah* of *Keter*, since they express the will and desire of the Almighty and are therefore higher than the Torah, which embodies the Divine wisdom (in the same way that, in the human being, will and desire are rooted higher in the psyche than intellectual understanding). Fulfilment of the commandments and prayer restore the broken connections in the higher worlds, allowing Divine Light to come into our world, and increasing its exposure. According to Kabbalah, by fulfilling the commandments a person 'raises up the female waters' (*mayin nukvin* – ascent of the holy sparks, fallen from the world of *Tohu* as a result of the shattering of the holy vessels) – i.e. the striving of Creation to unite with God – which leads to the restoration of the connection between the *sefirah* of *Malchut* (*nukva*) and *Zeir Anpin* (the six lower *sefirot*). This, in turn, leads to the restoration of connections between *Zeir Anpin* and the *partzufim Abba* and *Imma*, as a result of which an abundance of Divine Light (*mayin dechurin*) is attracted into the world. A person who breaks the commandments, on the other hand, brings about broken connections in the higher worlds, reduces the influx of Divine Light, and strengthens *sitra achra*.

Prayer has a special significance in the process of *tikun*. Prayers were introduced by sages after the destruction of the Temple, and they were intended to replace sacrifices. Let us attempt to understand why. The Temple was a single, complete channel that stretched from the lower to the very highest worlds. Offerings in the Temple (inanimate matter, plants, animals and incense) passed through the entire chain of worlds to the level of *Adam Kadmon*, which connected it to the single whole. With the destruction of the Temple, this channel was also destroyed. Prayers spoken with deep spiritual purpose were called upon to fulfil the same function of restoring the broken connections of the worlds. However, prayers cannot be considered the full equivalent of offering sacrifices, since only in the case of the most righteous do they reach the world of *Atzilut*, while for some people they never even leave the confines of our world, *Asiyah*.

## CONTINUOUS CREATION

The theory of continuous creation is one of the central moments in Judaism. It means that *Ein Sof* never stops creating worlds. In the event that the act of creation stops even for a single moment, all worlds would cease to exist and would dissolve into *Ein Sof*.

## A MEASURING ROD

In the book *Torah Or*, Alter Rebbe describes the concept of *botzina deqardinuta* (the measuring rod). Its philosophical meaning is as follows. From the phrase: 'How great are Your works, O Lord! You have made them all with wisdom (*Chochma*)' (*Tehillim*, 104:24), Alter Rebbe concludes that *Chochma* carries within it the quality of *Gevurah*, which, in turn, corresponds to the ability to show every form with all its features, since the quality of *Gevurah* (judgement) signifies the limits of all things. The Alter Rebbe writes: '*Botzina deqardinuta,* called a measuring rod or ruler in the *Zohar*, is the spiritual root of *chochma* in the world of *Atzilut*' [10]. Hence, in my opinion, it is possible to conclude that our world was created with the help of a measuring rod, and is therefore finite. It does not contain the infinite magnitudes. According to Kabbalah, the measuring rod is *Gevurah Atik*, the upper part of the *sefirah* of *Keter* of the world of Atzilut.

## THE CONCEPT OF *RATZO* AND *SHOV*

The concept of *ratzo* and *shov* (ebb and flow) signifies two movements in opposite directions. *Ratzo* is the striving of the human soul to be united with the Almighty. *Shov* is the returning of the soul, and the attraction of light from the Almighty towards a person.

At this point, I will end this short introduction to Kabbalah, and move on to describing a few approaches to the theory of information and quantum physics.

# A FEW APPROACHES TO THE THEORY OF INFORMATION AND QUANTUM PHYSICS

Before we begin the discussion on information, a definition of this concept is required. However, we encounter a few difficulties at this point.

## THE MEANING OF THE CONCEPT OF 'INFORMATION'

The American engineer Claude Shannon (1916–2001), the founder of information theory, wrote that 'the word "information" means different things to different scientists. It is hardly possible to expect that a single understanding of the word "information" would be satisfactory in order to use the term in all fields of science.' However, over the last three decades, specialists in different areas of information science have adopted the so-called general definition of information that 'data is meaning'. This can now be formulated in the following way:

• Information consists of one or more pieces of data.

• Data should be well formed (they should correspond to the language and rules of the chosen system).

• Formed data must have meaning.

The above definition, in turn, requires a definition of the concept of 'data'. Within information theory, data is defined as follows:

• Data is the absence of uniformity in the real world.

• Data is the absence of uniformity in the perception of two physical states.

• Data is the absence of uniformity between two symbols (for example, between the letters A and B).

There are a few properties of data that I consider necessary to include in this chapter. They are as follows:

• Information can consist of various types of data (primary, secondary, derivative, etc.).

• Information cannot exist without data representation.

• Information cannot exist without physical implementation.[31]

### EXCHANGE OF INFORMATION

Wheeler's[32] concept of 'It from bit' applies to information theory. It means that every particle – field or force, space-time etc. – functions in its own way, has its own meaning, and its existence is based on 'yes' and 'no' answers to questions (binary selection, i.e. bits). Therefore, it follows that the reality of our physical world is based on a non-material source, which is based on information. More and more scientists are coming to the conclusion that the basis of our reality is not matter and energy, but information [17].

The exchange of information in the simplest case can be described as the interaction between a subject and an object that are connected by a particular information channel. Thus, the following should be noted:

• The exchange of information is always mutual. A subject cognises an object, and at the same time the object cognises the subject.

• The quality of the exchange of information depends on the purity of the channel.

During the information exchange process, an information deficit occurs. Let us explain this in more detail. If all the internal information of object E

---

31 Implementation is practical realisation, i.e. the implementation of some kind of theory, agreement, law or idea. The verb 'implement' means 'to put into practice'. In programming, implementation generally means the expression of some kind of algorithm or function in programme code.

32 John Achibald Wheeler (1911–2008) – an American theoretical physicist, and member of the US National Academy of Sciences from 1952. In 1966 he became President of the American Physical Society. In 1990, Wheeler proposed that information is a fundamental concept in physics. According to his concept *It from bit*, all things physical are information-theoretic in origin.

is to be noted, and the information received by the subject about the object is E1, then the difference between E1 and E is the information deficit. For example, if we look at a stone, we can see its colour and form, but we will not be able to determine its chemical composition, or the energy of its atoms and molecules. Therefore, our information deficit is huge.

In 1948, Claude Shannon developed a mathematical theory of communication in order to express information in quantitative units. This is a rather vast question. Let us pause to look at just a few aspects of it.

**SHANNON'S ENTROPY**

The main concept in Shannon's theory is the unpredictability of information, or Shannon's entropy. It is expressed in this formula: $\log_2(N)$, where N is the system's number of possible states. Let us explain this with a simple example. Take a coin with two 'heads'. No matter how many times we toss it, it will always land heads up. In this case, the number of possible states is equal to one, therefore Shannon's entropy is equal to zero. This means that the informational uncertainty is equal to zero, and we are fully informed about the result of the toss. In the case of a coin with a head and a tail, the number of possible states is two. In this case, Shannon's entropy is equal to one. That is, one bit. In this situation, our informational uncertainty is equal to one bit. Our level of informedness is reduced correspondingly. When throwing a six-sided die, for example, our informational uncertainty increases and is equal to 2.58 bits.

Of course, information theory is now a very broad-ranging branch of science, and an interested reader can find information about it from the available literature. However, for the purposes of this book, I consider the brief summary above to be sufficient.

PHASE SPACE

Phase space is used in classical and quantum physics to describe the evolution of a system. Let us look at a simple example. One classical particle has three spatial coordinates – e.g. X1, X2 and X3 – and three impulse coordinates – P1, P2 and P3. Thus, the behaviour of one particle can be described in six-dimensional phase space. Correspondingly, the behaviour of a cluster of n particles can be described in phase space by the dimensionality 6n. For example, for a room full of molecules of gas, the dimensionality of phase space is equal to $10^{27}$ degrees. Each point of phase space describes the full state of a particular physical system. That is, each point of phase space corresponds to a vector. There is a multitude of theorems describing phase space [5]. (An interested reader can study this from the scientific literature available.)

## ENTROPY

All the main physics equations are symmetric in time; in other words, they permit movement backwards in time. There is only one law that is asymmetric in time – the Second Law of Thermodynamics. It says: 'In a closed system, entropy can remain constant or increase.' What exactly is entropy?

In physics, this concept is defined as a measure of a system's evident disorder. Let us look at an example used by Roger Penrose[33] in his book *The Emperor's New Mind*. Imagine a glass of water standing on the very edge of a table. If it is pushed slightly, it will fall onto the floor. The glass will break into pieces, and the water will spill out. In this situation, our glass of water follows Newton's physics equations. Now let us rewind this scene. Newton's laws do not prevent the broken pieces of glass from being collected up and reformed into a glass into which water is poured again, so that the full glass can jump back onto the edge of the table. However, this will never happen, although there is an infinitely small possibility that it could. The reason we will not observe the reverse process in reality is that the thermal movement of atoms in the fragments of glass and in the water is completely chaotic. It would require incredibly precise coordination of their movements in order to restore the glass with all the water collected back into it, and then throw it back up onto the table. Such coordination could only occur as the result of an incredible coincidence, which would be nothing short of miraculous. This illustrates the Second Law of Thermodynamics: the broken glass and spilled water are in a state of greater entropy (with considerable evident disorder) than the full glass on the table [5]. The mathematical definition of entropy is: entropy equals $S = k \log N$, where k is the Boltzmann constant, and N is the number of possible states in the system. Entropy is proportionate to the volume of the range of the system's states in phase space.

It is interesting and also very important to note that thermodynamic

---

33 Roger Penrose (born 1931, England) – a physician and mathematician who worked in various fields of mathematics, and originator of Twistor Theory. He was a respected professor in many foreign universities and academies. In 1989 his book *The Emperor's New Mind* was published, in which he outlined the theory of so-called strong artificial intelligence, explaining how it cannot be realised. He was knighted in 1994 for outstanding services to the development of science.

entropy and Shannon's informational entropy use the same concept of the
number of possible states. The famous physicist Jacob Bekenstein[34] wrote
that 'Thermodynamic entropy and Shannon entropy are conceptually equivalent: the number of arrangements that are counted by Boltzman entropy
reflects the amount of Shannon information one would need to implement
any particle arrangement'.

## A FEW CONCEPTS OF QUANTUM PHYSICS

Quantum physics developed in the early 20th century and is now one of
the most successful theories of physics describing our world. Despite the
fact that quantum physics makes correct predictions that are confirmed by
means of experiments, debate about its philosophical basis continues to this
day. Let us examine the principal differences between quantum and classical
physics. (By 'classical physics', we mean physics as described by the laws of
Newton and Einstein.)

In classical physics, a particle possesses properties of reality and locality
(separability). This means that a particle exists independently of our observations. If we know the original position and speed of a particle, as well as
the forces acting upon it, then we can calculate with absolute accuracy its
possible evolution in time and space.

The principal difference of quantum physics is that a quantum particle
(entity) can behave like both a particle and a wave. According to Heisenberg's
uncertainty principle, it is impossible to simultaneously determine the precise spatial coordinates and impulse of a particle, or energy and time..

Before the moment of measurement, a quantum particle exists in a state
of superposition, i.e. in many places at once. The state of such a particle is
described by Schrödinger's wave function, intended to determine the probability of the location of a particle at a given moment.

However, as a result of measurement, the situation suddenly changes.
From the quantum state of superposition, a particle jumps over to a classic
state with definite coordinates (collapse of the quantum state). It is impossible to calculate to which classical state the superposition will collapse. We
can only calculate probabilities. There are many explanations (interpretations) for this process and I will return to these later. The process of a

---

34  Jacob Bekenstein (1947–2015) – a theoretical physicist who first postulated that black holes can
have entropy.

jump-like change in a system during measuring, as described above, is one of the central problems of quantum physics, and it is called the 'problem of measurement'.

The situation described above is illustrated by what has become a classic 'double slit experiment'. Its essence is as follows. One photon is fired in the direction of a plate with two slits, behind which there is a screen. It might seem that the photon would pass through one slit or the other. The screen should record the photon's maximum number of arrivals at each slit. In fact, this is not the case. A picture appears on the screen, showing interference – that is, the evenly alternating maximum and minimum arrival points of photons. This demonstrates that the photon actually passes through both slits at the same time, behaving like a wave.

If, in this same experiment, photon detectors are placed in the slits, the behaviour of the photon changes drastically. In this case, the photon passes through one slit or the other, like a classic particle. This creates the impression that the photon flying towards the plate knows in advance that it is going to be measured in the slit. There is no fully adequate explanation for this, but there are a variety of interpretations. Let us briefly look at a few of these:

• The Copenhagen interpretation. In brief, this concept concludes that reality occurs only as a result of measurement. Before measurement, it is not possible to talk about objective reality.

• The 'many-worlds' interpretation proposed by Hugh Everett,[35] which says that, during measurement, all possible results are realised, although in different worlds, and we receive a single result, which corresponds with our world.

• There are also other interpretations, in particular the modal, ensemble and 'hidden variables', but I will not examine these in detail.

Another possible explanation for the problem of measurement is the process of decoherence.[36] In fact, during the measurement process, a quantum

---

35  Hugh Everett (1930–1982) – an American physicist and founder of the quantum theory of parallel worlds. Hugh Everett was the first scientist to propose the many-worlds interpretation of quantum mechanics, which he called 'relativity of states'.

36  Decoherence is the exchange of informations systems with the loss of information in the environment. For more information on decoherence, see pages 29, 50, 74 and 119.

particle gives out information about its location to the observer, which is an irreversible process. From my point of view, this explanation is one of the closest to the objective.

The decoherence hypothesis makes it possible to answer the second important question of quantum physics, which can be formulated as follows:

'Why do macroscopic objects, which are made up of quantum particles – electrons, protons etc. – demonstrate classical and not quantum properties?'

According to the decoherence hypothesis, this also occurs as a result of the loss of information from the system in the environment. It is important to note that the hypothesis of decoherence has not been definitively proven. There are also other theories (for example, de Broglie-Bohm's pilot wave theory, gravitational collapse theory, etc.).

In the book *The Outer Limits of Reason* Noson S. Yanofsky describes a 'quantum eraser' experiment, which is the modification of the 'double slit' experiment described above. Its essence is that behind the slits there is a diagonal polarisation filter that can be moved away from the screen quickly. Scientists developed a technique that allows removing it after the photon has passed through the slit. The results of the experiment showed that the photon changes its behaviour retrospectively. There are two possible explanations to that. Either by moving the polarisation filter the experimenter amends the past or the photon 'knows' what he is going to do. This conclusion is mind-bending. I think we can derive a possible explanation from the Wholeness Postulate, which states that the outcome of the experiment depends on the whole setup of the experiment (including the experimenter). We will discuss this later.

### QUANTUM ENTANGLEMENT

As noted above, classical systems possess the properties of reality and location (separability). The term 'entanglement' was introduced by Austrian physicist Erwin Schrödinger in 1935. Its essence is as follows. If there are two particles that have interacted with each other and are then separated by any distance (up to the size of the universe), the measurement of the properties of one particle (for example, the polarisation of a photon) will accurately predict the measurement of the same property for the second particle. In fact, a 100 per cent correlation is observed here. Together with his colleagues Boris Podolsky and Nathan Rosen, Albert Einstein wrote a paper on the issue (the EPR paradox), calling entanglement 'a spooky action at a distance'. He believed that quantum theory was incomplete, and there is a more general or more fundamental theory that can explain this correlation. In fact, quantum entanglement could be explained in the following ways:

• A certain interaction that has spread faster than the speed of light. (Not registered.)

• The existence of hidden parameters and variables. (Not clarified.)

• The manipulation of the experimenter's free will. (Unproven.)

In 1964, Irish physicist John Bell proved a theorem that 'put an end' to locality in quantum mechanics. Consequently, many physics experiments proved the existence of entanglement between quantum particles. In particular, in one such experiment on the Canary Islands, photons were separated from each other by a distance of 147 kilometres (91 miles), and a 100 per cent correlation was established between the measurements. Thus, the non-locality (inseparability) of quantum systems was proven. This means that the properties of a system depend not only on its place and position in space, but also on the quantum correlation with other systems any distance from it.

## QUANTUM INFORMATION

In quantum theory, information is a quantitative value characterising a system [1]. The essence of quantum information, and also its exclusive characteristic, is the fact that this physical value could not be better suited to the role of the primary substance of all things. More and more theoreticians believe that the key idea leading to the great unification of all things can become a reformulation of views on nature, not in terms of material and energy, but in terms of information. The first to promote this idea was the great American physicist John Archibald Wheeler (it was he who founded the concept of It from bit). The English physicist Paul Davies expressed his support of Wheeler in an article, stating: 'Normally we think of the world as composed of simple, clodlike, material particles, and information as a derived phenomenon attached to special, organised states of matter. But maybe it is the other way around: perhaps the universe is really a frolic of primal information, and material objects a complex secondary manifestation.' Quantum information cannot be destroyed, copied or cloned. Quantum information is itself a physical entity and exists even when a system is in a non-local state – in a different reality. Therefore, it can be considered a primary substance from which local objects can manifest themselves during the process of decoherence. In closed quantum systems (pure states) the measurement of information is equal to one – that is, for any isolated system, the maximum information is equal to one. In mixed states (open systems), information is less than one, since it is lost as a consequence of the process of decoherence.

It was noted above that classic information is measured in bits. Quantum information is measured in Qubits. There is a principal difference. In classic computing, two states are possible – zero or one. A Qubit is understood as a binary quantum system. Any quantum system can be represented as a set of an unlimited quantity of Qubits. The difference between a Qubit and its classic analogue is that the number of states in a quantum two-level system is infinite. In each definite moment of time, information taken from the Qubit is equal to one 'classic' bit.

At present, Qubit theory is based around the development of quantum computers whose capabilities will exponentially[37] surpass the abilities of classical computers. The fundamental idea of a quantum computer is the creation of a Qubit system in a coherent state,[38] and the management of such a system with the help of special quantum algorithms.

## PHASE SPACE IN QUANTUM MECHANICS

Unlike classical systems, quantum systems can be in an infinite quantity of states. Such systems are described by Hilbert's[39] infinite-dimensional space. A vector at a point in this space characterises the state of a closed quantum system.

With this, I conclude the introductory section of this book, which gives a brief glimpse of the main concepts of Kabbalah, information theory and quantum physics. The interested reader can make use of the myriad scientific literature to develop a much deeper understanding. However, I hope that this introduction is sufficient for our continued journey through the pages of this book.

---

37  Exponentially. Used here in the sense of 'sharply', or 'significantly'.

38  Coherent state – the state of a quantum system whose properties are as close as possible to a classical state.

39  David Hilbert (1862–1943) – a German universal mathematician who made a significant contribution to the development of many areas of mathematics. Between 1910 and 1920 he was recognised as a world leader among mathematicians. Hilbert developed a wide spectrum of fundamental ideas in many fields of mathematics, including the first full axiomatisation of Euclidean geometry and the theory of Hilbert spaces.

*Chapter 1*

# CREATION

## 1.1 CREATION OUT OF NOTHING (EX NIHILO)

The concept of creation out of nothing is one of the cornerstones of Judaism. It is mentioned in the book *Sefer Yetzirah*. The fullest 'pre-Kabbalist' foundation of this concept is introduced by Saadia Gaon in *The Book of Beliefs and Opinions*. His explanations are sufficiently simple. If we assume that worlds are created out of something, then the question arises as to what this 'something' was itself created from. As a result, we end up with an infinite regression, which is absurd. If we suppose that worlds are created from something that was not created by the Almighty, then that means that God has no authority over it, which is an unacceptable limitation of His powers [23]. Later, Kabbalists studying the system of worlds and *sefirot* were faced with the problem of what to accept as 'nothing'. Opinion was divided. Nachmanides believed that everything came from God's absolute 'nothing'. Rabbi Abraham ben David believed that 'nothing' is the *sefirah* of *Keter*. Some Kabbalists have defined 'nothing' as symbolising a reality that the human intellect is incapable of understanding.

In fact, the concept of nothing is beyond human comprehension. One of the greatest Greek philosophers of the pre-Socratic era, Parmenides of Elea, stated that it is not possible to think about nothing because it cannot exist.

## 1.2 THE CREATION OF INFORMATION

As mentioned earlier, in the book *Sefer Yetzirah* it is maintained that everything was created out of the twenty-two letters of the sacred language and the ten *sefirot*, which are called numbers. Both letters and numbers are an informational code. In the book *Torah Or*, it says that the spiritual root of the letters is the *sefirah* of *Keter*, which is higher than the *sefirah* of *Chochma* [10]. The whole world was created by means of the ten utterances of the Almighty ('Let there be light…' etc.). These utterances are functional informational commands. From the description of the process of *tzimtzum* (see *Introduction to Kabbalah*) we can make an inference that the only 'building material' for everything that exists is God's light (information). We can state that all the reality, including worlds, *sefirot*, souls, matter, consists of different representations of God's light (information). According to the teaching of Arizal, even an inanimate object – a stone, for example – has a soul and a spiritual life force. 'The "soul" of the object is the sequence of letters, deriving from the ten utterances of the Almighty, that invest themselves within the object and impart existence and vitality to it, allowing it to manifest as existence from non-existence and the void that was before the six days of creation' [8].

Modern science is gradually coming to the conclusion that the basis of our perceived reality is not matter and energy, but information. The information of a quantum system cannot be copied or destroyed. One of the greatest physicists of the 20th century, John Archibald Wheeler, wrote: 'It is not unreasonable to imagine that information sits at the core of physics, just as it sits at the core of a computer. It from bit.' In other words, everything in existence – every particle, every force field, and even the space-time continuum itself – is given its own function, its own purpose and, ultimately, its own existence – even if in some situations this is indirect – from the answers to the questions that we pose with the help of physical equipment, and which propose a 'yes' or 'no' answer, from binary alternatives, or bits.

Wheeler also wrote: '*It from bit* symbolizes the idea that every item of the physical world has at its bottom – a very deep bottom, in most instances – an immaterial source and explanation; the idea that what we call reality arises in the last analysis from the posing of yes-no questions and the registering of equipment-evoked responses; in short, the idea that all things physical are information-theoretic in origin and this is a participatory universe.'

Wheeler proposed that information is fundamental to the physics of the universe. Philosopher David Chalmers wrote: 'In the light of the notion of "It from bit", the laws of physics can be expressed in terms of information that confirms different states, giving rise to different effects without explaining the nature of the state. The only thing that matters is their position in informational space. If this is so, then information is also a natural candidate for the role of the fundamental theory of consciousness. We are approaching the concept of reality, according to which information is truly fundamental and possesses two basic aspects connecting the physical and perceived sides of reality.'

Listed below, in the form of hypotheses, are several propositions that I consider to be crucial to this book.

• Creation – the creation by *Ein Sof* of information, and then its distribution and formation with the ultimate goal of the creation of man.

• Spiritual worlds – the *sefirot*, light, all souls, angels, and all the entities of the material world, including humans, are informational entities.

• According to the intention of Creation, there must be a continuous, mutual exchange of information between the expression of *Ein Sof* within the system of *sefirot*, and man.

• As a key participant in the mutual exchange of information, man is given great authority over Creation.

• The light of *sovev* (see Introduction, page 15) is the information about the existence of *Ein Sof*, which cannot be perceived by Creation. The light of *memalei* is information about the expression of *Ein Sof* in the system of *sefirot*.

• A *sefirah* is an informational entity (called a 'vessel') – for example, *Gevurah* (contraction, judgement, power) – comprising information about the existence of *Ein Sof* and information about the expression of *Ein Sof* within the system of *sefirot*.

• *Hishtalshelut* is the concealment of information by means of its transfer into other forms as it is spread throughout the worlds. The greatest concealment of information occurs in our world, *Asiyah*.

• In the world of *Atzilut*, 'light and vessels are as one': that is, both informational components of the *sefirot* are in full harmony with each other. In the world of *Beriah*, information about the properties of vessels begins to prevail over information about the expression of *Ein Sof* in the system of worlds (vessel over light). This makes the formation of other informational entities

(souls, archangels, *Gan Eden*) possible. In the world of *Yetzirah,* this prevalence is increased, thus enabling the emergence of a great many information
entities (souls, angels). In the world of *Asiyah,* this prevalence reaches its
maximum, making the creation of the material world and man possible.

The thesis of a continuous mutual exchange of information can be derived from
the analysis of the first verse of the book *Sefer Yetzirah.* As written in the book
*Sefer Yetzirah, the Book of Creation In Theory and Practice* by Aryeh Kaplan:

With 32 mystical paths of Wisdom
    Engraved *Yah*
        The Lord of Hosts
        The God of Israel
    The living God
        King of the Universe
    *El Shaddai*
        Merciful and Gracious
        High and Exalted
        Dwelling in eternity
        Whose name is Holy –
          He is lofty and holy –
And He created His universe
    With three books
        With text
        With number
        And with Communication

According to commentary given by Aryeh Kaplan, *Yah* – the letter *Yud*
corresponds to *sefirah Chochma,* letter *Heh* to *sefirah Binah.* 'The Lord of
Hosts' corresponds to the *sefirot Netzah* and *Hod.* 'God of Israel' is con-
nected to 'The Lord of Hosts'. 'The living God' corresponds to the *sefirah
Yesod.* 'King of the Universe' to the last *sefirah* of *Malkhut.* Here we can see
that the movement goes top to bottom and latter we will see it go bottom to
top. '*El Shaddai*' translated as 'Almighty God' also corresponds to the *sefirah
Yesod.* 'Merciful and Gracious' corresponds to the *sefirot Chesed, Gevurah,
Tiferet, Netzach* and *Hod.* 'High and Exalted' corresponds to *sefirah Binah.*
'Dwelling in Eternity' corresponds to the *sefirah Chochma.* 'His Name is
Holy' corresponds to the highest *sefirah Keter.*

## 1.3 CREATION AND THE SECOND LAW OF THERMODYNAMICS

First of all, let us recall the concept of informational entropy, as proposed by Claude Shannon (see Introduction, page 24). The greater the informational entropy,[40] the less we are informed, and vice versa.

• For us, *Ein Sof* is unknowable. It is beyond the limits of our intellect. In the book *Tikunei Zohar Patach Eliyahu*, it says: 'You are wise, but not with any knowable wisdom.' This means that the wisdom of *Ein Sof* differs from human wisdom not by its level, but by its quality, and it cannot be defined. Thus, our informational entropy (uncertainty) concerning *Ein Sof* stretches to infinity.

• *Tzimtzum* in its direct sense means the contraction and formation of an empty spherical space into which a ray of light is subsequently emitted. According to the concept of Alter Rebbe, *tzimtzum* should not be understood literally. It interprets the concept of empty space as a space with a very little amount of residual light (*reshimu*), where a thin ray of light was radiated. It is worth pointing out two facts. Firstly, *tzimtzum* is the primary information that we receive about the action of *Ein Sof,* and secondly, *tzimtzum* permits very little variation. Thus, the informational entropy (uncertainty) of *tzimtzum* tends, but is not equal to zero. *Tzimtzum* corresponds to the world of *Gevurah* (contraction).

• It is important to note that 'before' *tzimtzum*, information did not exist as we have no information about *Ein Sof*. Hence we can consider *tzimtzum* the first created information.

Here, at the very beginning of Creation, God introduced the Second Law of Thermodynamics. The low entropy world of *tzimtzum* evolved into the high entropy world of *Adam Kadmon*.

• *Adam Kadmon* proceeds from the state of *tzimtzum* as a result of the expansion (*Chesed*). Although the structure of *Adam Kadmon* resembles the outline of a person on the outside, on the inside there is no kind of division and structurisation that would allow for a large number of variations of the

_____

40 Entropy is the uncertainty of a system's state. – *Author's note.*

```
                              ○
                              ↓
                              ○
                              ↓
                              ○
                              ↓
                              ○
                              ↓
                              ○
                              ↓
                              ○
                              ↓
                              ○
                              ↓
                              ○
                              ↓
                              ○
                              ↓
                              ○
```

Fig. 2. The structure of the world of *Tohu*

states. Thus, the informational entropy of the world of *Adam Kadmon* is sufficiently great.

• The world of *Akudim* is formed as a result of the merging of the ten *sefirot* into one vessel. Although the *sefirot* are not separate from each other, the world of *Akudim* is more structured than the world of *Adam Kadmon*. Its informational entropy is less than in the world of *Adam Kadmon*.

• The world of *Nekudim (Tohu)* is formed from the world of *Akudim*. In the book *Torah Or*, it is written: 'From the world of *Akudim* comes the world of *Nekudim* where each *sefirah* exists separately; therefore, the ten *sefirot* of this world are called the ten points.'

This means that the *sefirot* have undergone a significant descent from the level of the ten *sefirot* of the *Akudim*. Therefore, the *Chochma* of this world can be called 'knowable wisdom' [9]. Thus, the world of *Nekudim (Tohu)* represents the ten barely interacting *sefirot* stretched out in a line

(Fig. 2). There are almost no variations here. Consequently, the informational entropy of the world of *Tohu* tends to zero. Just as with *tzimtzum*, the world of *Tohu* is the world of *Gevurah*.

As already mentioned in the Introduction, the 'shattering of vessels' took place in the world of *Tohu*.

Let us attempt to understand why this happened.

The Kabbalist definition of the cause of the 'shattering of vessels' is 'strong light – weak vessels'. This means that the information about the characteristics of the Almighty (the vessel) was expressed very weakly in comparison with the information about *Ein Sof* in the system of *sefirot*. Consequently, a transformation of the information system occurred (the shattering of separate entities in which the 'fragments of the vessels' contained 'sparks of light'). In other words, entities were formed, in which information about the 'self' significantly prevailed over information about God. These very 'fragments' served as the embryos of the formation of entities with their own 'self'. These fragments enabled the emergence of *sitra achra*, since its main characteristic is the prevalence of information about the 'self' over information about the Almighty [9]. Alter Rebbe wrote: 'It is known that the shattering of the vessels took place in the world of *Nekudim*, also known as the world of *Tohu*. This occurred because the "spotted" *sefirot* of the world of *Nekudim* existed separately, on their own, and were not prepared to interact.'

From my point of view, the 'shattering of vessels' in the world of *Tohu* was caused by the Second Law of Thermodynamics in action. Here we observe the transition from the state of very low entropy (*sefirot* stretched in one line) to the state of high entropy, containing a huge amount of the fragments of the vessels in a chaotic state.

• The world of *Atzilut*. Here, the *sefirot* are presented in the form of *partzufim* – configurations – and interact with each other. Each *sefirah* of the world of *Atzilut* contains another ten *sefirots* and so on. In fact, the concept of the fractal[41] is introduced here. Many natural objects possess the properties of fractals: coastlines, clouds, the tops of trees, snowflakes, the circulatory system, etc.

---

41 Fractal – a mathematical figure that possesses the property of likeness. (An object exactly or almost exactly resembling a part of itself, i.e. the whole has the same form as one or more of its parts.) The term 'fractal' was introduced by Benoit Mandelbrot in 1975.

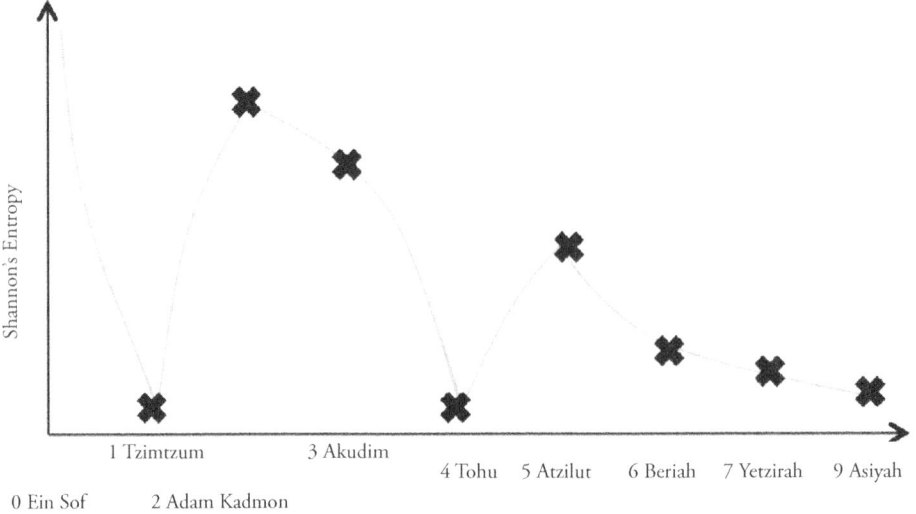

Fig. 3. Graph showing the informational entropy of the worlds

However, let us return to the world of *Atzilut*. Unlike in the world of *Tohu*, the *sefirot* interact with each other in *Atzilut*, as a result of which their fractal structure has a large number of combinations of the ten *sefirot*. The informational entropy of this world is great, although it is less than in the world of *Akudim*, where the *sefirot* are merged into a single whole.

• The world of *Beriah*. The structure of the *sefirot* in the world of *Beriah* is analogous with the structure of the *sefirot* in the world of *Atzilut*, although, as mentioned earlier, there are other informational entities in the world of *Beriah* (archangels, souls, *Gan Eden*). Therefore, *Beriah* is more ordered than *Atzilut*, and its informational entropy is lower than that of *Atzilut*.

• The world of *Yetzirah*. The tendency towards increasing orderliness continues. As mentioned earlier, there is a large number of angels and souls in *Yetzirah*. Consequently, its informational entropy is lower than that of *Beriah*.

• The world of *Asiyah* (our material world). Compared with the worlds of *Atzilut, Beriah* and *Yetzirah*, orderliness reaches its maximum in the world of *Asiyah*, since it contains a large number of low-entropy structures. Therefore, the informational entropy of the world of *Asiyah* in the *Atzilut-Beriah-Yetzirah-Asiyah* system is minimal. This corresponds to the modern scientific concept, which says that the initial state of our universe (at the moment of the Big Bang) was a very low entropy state. The world of *Asiyah* is also the world of *Gevurah*.

The results of this analysis are shown in Fig. 3.

Some rather interesting conclusions can be drawn from this:

1. The process of creation is governed by the Second Law of Thermodynamics, introduced by God at the very beginning.

2. The process of creation (the dissemination of information) is of a cyclical nature. The cycle of *Gevurah* (contraction) is replaced by the cycle of *Chesed* (expansion). This can be compared to a person breathing in and out. We can find confirmation of this in the book *Sefer Yetzirah*, where it says that the *sefirot* 'run and return' according to the word of the Almighty [4].

3. All the worlds of *Gevurah* (*tzimtzum*, *Tohu* and *Asiyah*) are highly ordered and possess very low informational entropy.

1.4 CONTINUOUS CREATION

One of the main ideas of Judaism and Kabbalah is that God continuously transforms nothing into something. Many scientists state that the thermodynamical entropy of nothing is infinite. If we assume that the notion of thermodynamical entropy is applicable to the state of nothing, we can consider the process of creation as a transformation, from a state of infinite entropy to a state of finite entropy. According to the laws of physics, this kind of transformation must be continuously supported. If the support stops even for a moment, the reverse process will take place and something will become nothing.

1.5 KABBALAH, TIME AND SPACE

Despite the millennia of debates, time remains the most mysterious concept in physics. Opinions range from time being a fundamental property of our reality to time being a psychological construct of our minds. Time is interpreted differently in general relativity and quantum mechanics. In the former, time is part of the system that is space-time. In the latter, time is external to the system, like a clock ticking outside. The question is, why does the arrow of time, which transports us from the past into the present and then the future, exist? Why does it not work the other way around? All the laws of physics are time symmetrical, apart from one: the Second Law of Thermodynamics, which states that in a closed system entropy must either remain the same or increase. Many scientists have concluded that this is the law that explains why there is an arrow of time; however, there is no final consensus.

Everybody agrees, though, that time is change. We perceive this change through the flow of information in the opposite direction, from the future into the present, and the present into the past, at which point it becomes fixed and unchangeable. Our uncertainty about the future is large; therefore, Shannon's entropy is also large. At the same time, we know everything about the past, which is fixed, which means that Shannon's entropy is equal to zero. We can now rephrase the question of why there is an arrow of time in the following way: why is there an arrow of information moving from the future into the now and then the past? To answer this question from the perspective of Kabbalah, please see chapter 1.3. The degree of our uncertainty about *Ein Sof*, and hence Shannon's entropy, is infinitely large. All of Creation is a dynamic flow of information from *Ein Sof* into the system of worlds. Therefore, according to the Kabbalah, *Ein Sof* constantly upholds all of Creation. It is this flow of information from *Ein Sof* into the system of worlds that defines the arrow of time. At this point, the reader may point out that we are talking about time as a subjective experience of the individual; however, each proton, electron and every other particle and constituent of Creation is continually receiving information from *Ein Sof*, and therefore is subject to the same effect. From this we can infer that since the flow of information is present in all worlds, in one way or another time is also present in all of the worlds. And only *Ein Sof* is beyond time.

In his special theory of relativity Einstein did away with the notion of absolute time. He introduced the concept of space-time as a single whole. In Kabbalah, space is associated with *Zeir Anpin,* which includes six *sefirot* (see Introduction to Kabbalah), while time is associated with the *sefirah* of *Malchut. Zeir Anpin* and *Malchut* comprise an integral system with a continuous flow of information. Thus, Kabbalah provides us with the notion of space and time as a single whole.

In his general theory of relativity Einstein showed that there is an interaction between space, time and matter. In chapter 1.2 it was shown that the whole creation consists of information presented in different forms by God.

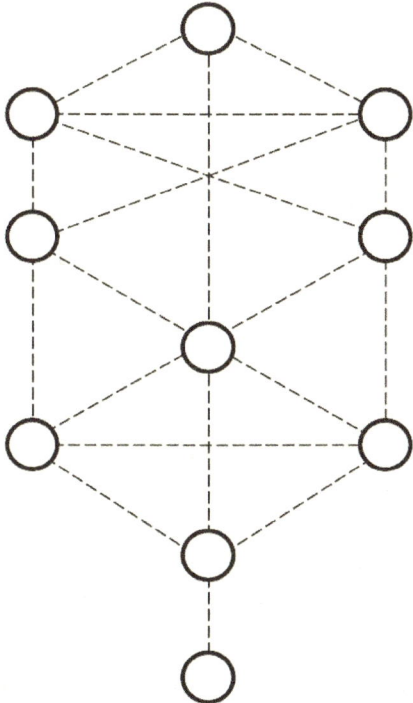

Fig. 4. The structure of the world of *Atzilut*

From here we can infer that the system space-time-matter is an informational entity. There is a question in science, which is formulated like this: will the time-space exist if all matter is removed? To answer this question, let's come back to the processes of *tzimtzum*, the first stage of creation described in chapter 1.3 and the introduction to Kabbalah. Let's remind the reader that the essence of *tzimtzum* is the creation by God of the 'empty' space (*tehiru*) as a result of the concealment of His light (information). But was it 'empty'? According to Kabbalah, *tehiru* contains residual light (information), called *reshimu*. From my point of view, the concept of *reshimu* means that there is no actual 'nothing' in the creation. It introduced the concept of the minimal level of information in the creation. The concept of *reshimu* resonates with the idea of quantum vacuum as an entity with the lowest possible energy, the 'ground state'. Quantum vacuum is considered by physicists as a 'background' which affects all the processes in our universe.

## 1.6 KABBALAH AND THE INTERNET

As shown above, the world of *Tohu* turned out to be unstable. This was reflected in the fact that every *sefirah* of the world of *Tohu* could transfer its influence only to one subsequent *sefirah* (Fig. 2).

At the same time, the world of *Atzilut* possesses much more stability, since every *sefirah* therein has many different ways of transferring its influence to other *sefirot* (Fig. 4).

In the 1960s, American scientists started to think about the effective use of computers, and began work on connecting computers on a general network. This was the beginning of the Internet era. However, in order to solve such a complex question, it was necessary to overcome many obstacles.

One of the stages was to develop an information communications network that would be stable and enable the transfer of information at a given speed and without distortion.

The solution came from an unexpected source. Polish émigré Paul Baran worked for the Rand Corporation, which carried out theoretical research, serving the US Department of Defense, among others. At that time, US anti-aircraft defence consisted of a network of radars that transmitted their data via telephone lines to a single command centre, where there was a computer to process the incoming information and issue instructions. Any breakdown in the communication system could lead to drastic consequences. Baran's job was to develop a more reliable version of the information communications system, which could continue to function even in the event of a nuclear attack.

At that time, the telephone communications system consisted of a series of relays, each of which transmitted an incoming signal onwards to the next strictly defined relay (Fig. 5).

Fig. 5. Telephone network where 'redundancy' (free capacity) is equal to 1

Fig. 6. Distribution network where 'redundancy' is equal to 4 or more

From a mathematical point of view, this system had a level of 'redundancy' equal to 1, and it was extremely unstable and vulnerable. Baran proposed a new form of communications networks, which were called distribution networks (Fig. 6).

In such networks, every distribution node was connected to another three or four nodes and could independently decide which channel to send information along. The level of redundancy in this system was 3 or 4, and it was extremely stable and effective [18].

Consequently, Baran's idea was used in the creation of ARPANET, the prototype for the modern-day Internet.

The reader can readily see a parallel between Baran's conclusions and the Kabbalist position on the structure of the worlds of *Tohu* and *Atzilut*.

Baran's second revolutionary idea was to divide messages into separate parts (packets); Tim Berners-Lee was working on a similar idea at the same time. As

a result of this division, the speedy, effective transmission of packets along separate channels became possible. After the packets arrived at a particular point,
the computer put them together and reassembled the original message.

The reader may quite rightly wonder: 'How does this relate to Kabbalah?'

There is, however, a very close similarity. The information that comes
through the *sefirah* of *Keter* is divided into parts and passes through the
whole system of *sefirot* by means of many different combinations, before
being joined together in the *sefirah* of *Malchut*.

*Chapter 2*

# THE ROLE OF MAN IN CREATION

Earlier, I explained that in the process of Creation, a key role was set for man, as man is a 'partner' of the Almighty in the informational process. This is also confirmed by the texts of the Torah. In his book *Torah Or*, the Alter Rebbe gave a commentary on extracts from the prayer *Shema Yisrael*: 'If you will diligently obey My commandments which I enjoin upon you this day, to love the L-rd your Gd and to serve Him with all your heart and with all your soul, I will give rain for your land at the proper time ... Take care lest your heart be lured away, and you turn astray and worship alien gods and bow down to them. For then the L-rd's wrath will flare up against you, and He will close the heavens so that there will be no rain...' The Alter Rebbe explains that the rain can be understood to represent light (information). From my point of view, worshipping alien gods is a person's refusal to participate with the Almighty in the information process [9]. In *Bereishit* (book of Genesis) it says: 'because the Lord God had not brought rain upon the earth, and there was no man to work the soil' (*Bereishit*, 2:5). In my opinion, this means that, during Creation, the full information process was formed only after man was created.

This is also borne out by the fact that here, for the first time in the Torah, the Almighty is presented to us as 'The Lord God' (*Havayah Elohim*), and not 'God' (*Elohim*) as up until this point in the Torah. As previously noted in 'A short introduction to Kabbalah', the name 'the Lord God' (*Havayah Elohim*) represents the whole system of *sefirot*. Therefore, only after the creation of man was the whole system of *sefirot* included in the exchange of information.

It is important to note that the whole of Creation takes part in the exchange of information (every proton, every neutron and every electron). However, the level at which these particles participate in the exchange of information is strictly measured and cannot be changed. Only to mankind did God give the ability to vary his participation in the exchange of information.

According to Kabbalah, mankind's main task is *tikun* – rectifying the situation that arose following the 'shattering of vessels' – and, ultimately, the destruction of *sitra achra*. At first this task was given to the first man. In the same chapter of *Bereishit* it says: 'Now the Lord God took the man, and He placed him in the Garden of Eden to work it and to guard it' (*Bereishit*, 2:15). The Alter Rebbe gives the following explanation for this verse: The word work suggests the fulfilling of the 248 positive commandments of the Torah, in order to attract eternal light into the Garden of Eden. If Adam had not sinned, then this powerful disclosure of Divine Light would have been sufficient to raise up the sparks of holiness which had fallen into the worlds of evil and mingled with them [9]. It should be pointed out that Adam could do this without special effort, as long as evil was separated from good.

Having eaten the forbidden fruit (which can be interpreted as receiving forbidden information about good and evil), Adam allowed evil into his heart. Thus, between the region of *sitra achra* and that of holiness, an intermediary region of *kelipat nogah* formed, which contained both good and evil. Hence, Adam did not only fail to complete the task he had been given, but he made it more complicated for himself and all his descendants who, to this day, must fight against the evil in their hearts. As a result of Adam's sin, the disclosure of Divine Light (the flow of information) was significantly reduced. Adam was banished to the material world so that he and his descendants could carry out their allotted task of fulfilling the commandments.

## 2.1 THE THEORY OF EVIL

A person is thus obliged to participate in an exchange of information with the Almighty, according to the laws established by Him, and thereby destroy evil. Consequently, a person's failure to participate in this process is evil. This situation requires further explanation.

People often ask questions such as: 'Why did the good God create evil?' 'Why is our world full of evil?' 'Why does God allow bad things to happen?'

Yet in the Talmud it says, 'Only good comes from God.'

It would seem that we are faced with a direct contradiction. But this is not the case.

Evil can be divided into two parts.

1. Evil towards individual entities (people, animals, plants).

2. Evil towards Creation as a whole.

Let us examine the first point. In *The Guide for the Perplexed,* Maimonides classes evil affecting the individual as follows:

• The evil a person experiences as a consequence of his own material nature (pain, illness, death).

• The evil one person inflicts upon another.

• The evil a person inflicts upon himself by doing that which he should not.

Maimonides gives a general definition of evil in relation to the individual as a lack or deficiency of some quality (life, health, wealth, happiness, etc) in that individual. Maimonides believes that the main cause of such deficiency is ignorance and lack of understanding. Similarly, Saadia Gaon suggests that the main causes of evil are ignorance, fear and greed [7, 23]. By analysing the above classification, the following explanation ensues.

The first man was created to be immortal. He knew neither illness nor death. The cause of illness and death is the material state that appeared as a result of the first man's sin. People's inflicting of evil upon each other is the consequence of their failure to fulfil the commandments and the laws of the Torah, which proscribe all forms of evil that could be inflicted upon a person. It is important to note that if all the people on our planet fulfilled the commandments and the laws of the Torah, the world would return to the state in which it existed before the sin of Adam. Evil would be separate from good and exist only in a potential state, never being realised.

It is important that the concept of evil between people should be described on a psychological level.

## 2.2 EVIL IN MENTAL SPACE

I suggest that the reader should recall the concept of phase space, as described in the Introduction (page 24). Phase space is multidimensional – in fact, infinite-dimensional – and a point or a vector within it fully describes the state of the system at that moment. Thus, the state of any isolated quantum system is described as a vector in Hilbert's infinite-dimensional space.

In this book, I propose to examine mental processes within the context of infinite-dimensional mental space – both in individual and in world-wide terms. A point in this individual mental space will fully determine a person's mental (spiritual) state at that moment in time. (We will return to this concept in more detail in subsequent chapters.) Hence, all individual mental spaces are subsystems of a worldwide mental space encompassing all spiritual worlds and *sefirot*, and, under certain conditions, those individual mental spaces can correlate and establish interaction among themselves. If some kind of interaction were to be observed by means of the correlation of mental spaces, then mental connections would occur that would be both active and passive, and strong and weak.

If a person last communicated with an acquaintance thirty years ago and has not seen or heard from him since, then the mental connection with that person is passive. Meanwhile, in the case of people with whom we talk and interact often, active mental connections are established. As a rule, the strongest mental connections are established with our close relatives. After that come friends, acquaintances and others. It is interesting to note that mental connections can also be established with material objects. For example, if a particular object is designated using the term 'my' (for example 'my phone'), then I have a mental connection with it. In this case, it can be stated that evil, as described by the commandments and laws of the Torah, is expressed in the severing of a person's mental connections. For example, in the event of the illness or, God forbid, the death of a close relative, the mental connection with this person is severed. If some kind of material object previously referred to as 'mine' is taken away or stolen from us, the mental connection with this object is severed. If we do evil, our mental connection with the Almighty is severed.

At the same time, kindness and good deeds, being the opposite of evil, re-establish severed mental connections and create new ones. Recent neuro-physiological research shows that each mental connection corresponds to a particular group of neurons. When a connection is broken, the functioning of the group of neurons and the transmission of signals therein is broken, and we experience physical suffering. With time, the group of neurons, now deprived of mental connections, breaks up. Hence the saying, 'time heals'.

Let us now continue our journey in the 'realm of evil'.

## 2.3 EVIL TOWARDS CREATION

As mentioned above, man is a key figure in Creation. In Judaism, there are various views on the influence of man on Creation. One thing that emerges is that by not carrying out the will of the Almighty – that is, by not participating in the informational process – a person has a negative influence on Creation as a whole. However, opinion is divided over the details relating to this.

According to one view, by committing evil and not obeying the laws and statutes of the Almighty, a person weakens the power of God. The sages suggested that the power of Divine attributes depends on the actions of man. According to the view of Rabbi Bahya ben Asher,[42] man's failure to carry out the will of Heaven leads to the Almighty being distanced from His attributes (the system of *sefirot*).

Rabbi Menahem Recanati,[43] a renowned medieval Kabbalist, believed that the whole system of *sefirot* can be destroyed and returned to its source, as a result of the sins of mankind [3]. Several Talmud sages have suggested that, because of the sins of mankind, the attribute of Divine Judgement is strengthened and the attribute of Divine Mercy is weakened. In the book *Torah Or*, Alter Rebbe interprets this question as follows. Referring to extracts from *Tikunei Zohar* – 'Eliyahu began…' and 'When You go away from them, they are left like bodies without souls' – the Alter Rebbe explains that sins can result in a state whereby Divine Light (information) is practically removed from the *sefirot* (*mochin de gadlut*). At this moment, lower knowledge (see Introduction, page 16), which differentiates between good and evil, seems to fall asleep, and higher knowledge, which makes no distinction between good and evil, rules over the world [10].

Fully agreeing with the opinions outlined above, I propose the addition

---

42 Rabbi Bahya ben Asher – a great Spanish Jewish sage and eminent Torah commentator in the 13th century. He was a pupil at the *yeshiva* (Talmudic institute) in Barcelona, headed by Rabbi Solomon ben Abraham Adret (Rashba).

43 Rabbi Menahem Recanati (1250–1310) – Torah expert and Kabbalist. Lived in Italy.

of another hypothesis. To this end, let us recall one of the main concepts
of Judaism and Kabbalah – the continuous nature of Creation. It suggests
that the Almighty is constantly carrying out Creation. If He stops even
for a moment, our material world and all the spiritual worlds will return
to their source and disappear. With regard to this, we can recall the words
of the *Sefir Yetzirah* on the *sefirot*: 'At the word of the Almighty they [the
*sefirot*] run and return.'

One of the explanations of the problem of measurement in quantum
physics is decoherence. It states that any quantum system is manifest in the
plane of existence as a result of the exchange of information with other systems. In the event that the exchange of information stops (recoherence), the
quantum system disappears from the plane of existence. The whole informational process of Creation can be seen as the exchange of information
within the system of '*Ein Sof* – spiritual worlds – mankind'. This informational exchange is supported from two sides: both *Ein Sof* and mankind. It
has already been mentioned that, even in the event of the most minimal
pause in Creation on the part of *Ein Sof*, all worlds will disappear. However,
the same can be said of mankind. When man's non-participation in the
informational process reaches a critical point, the exchange of information
(decoherence) could stop, and the worlds would disappear.

Where can we find confirmation of this? In the Torah, of course. The situation described above took place before the Great Flood. The level of sin was
approaching a critical point. The antediluvian people had not only sinned
against the Almighty, inflicting evil upon Creation as a whole, but they had
also sinned against each other. Their level of participation in the informational process was extremely low. The world was on the verge of disappearing.
In my opinion, this was why the Almighty took the unprecedented decision
to destroy antediluvian humanity for the sake of the salvation of the world.
We can find a comparable situation in the description of the destruction of
Sodom and Gomorrah. This was a kind of localised flood. Note that the
inhabitants of Canaan were idol-worshippers, meaning that they had sinned
against the Almighty. However, the inhabitants of these two cities had also
sinned against each other and persecuted their guests. Hence, their evil (their
degree of non-participation in the informational process) was also approaching a critical point, so they were destroyed. At the same time, it is worth
pointing out that the builders of the tower of Babylon, who had sinned
against God and effectively declared war on Him, were not destroyed, but
merely dispersed, since they had treated each other well and had not sinned

against each other. From this, it is possible to conclude that one person's evil towards another is a much greater sin than evil towards the Almighty.

## 2.4 THE TORAH AND THE COMMANDMENTS

In the Introduction (page 15), it was noted that the light of the Almighty (information about Him) reaches our world in an extremely concealed state, and it is incredibly difficult for an ordinary person to see God in the material world and understand how to serve Him properly. In order to explain to man about his role in Creation, the Almighty provided another, more revealed channel of information, which is known as the Torah. It contains a full description of the rules and instructions that a person must observe in order to fully participate in Creation, as well as for living a happy life. The root of the Torah lies in Supreme Wisdom (the *sefirah* of *Chochma* in the world of *Atzilut*). In the Torah, the Almighty speaks about himself directly and indirectly. He speaks directly in the first of the Ten Commandments: 'I am the Lord, your God, Who took you out of the land of Egypt, out of the house of bondage. You shall not have the gods of others in My presence' (*Shemot*, 20:1–2).

I understand indirect information to mean the hidden meanings of the Torah. It should be noted that the Torah is the only information in our world whose source is eternal. In the Torah there are 248 positive commandments and 365 negative ones, and by observing these, a person fulfils their role in Creation to the maximum extent. The commandments express the will of the Creator of worlds, and their root is higher than the root of the Torah itself – in the *sefirah* of *Keter* in the world of *Atzilut*. Following the destruction of the Temple in Jerusalem, the sages replaced some of the commandments in the Torah with prayers, in particular the commandments associated with sacrifices. Thus, by studying the Sacred Scripture, observing the commandments, laws and statutes, and by praying, a person is fulfilling the role in Creation given to him by the Almighty, as well as finding personal happiness and well-being. Fulfilling the three conditions shown above has a direct effect on the whole system of *sefirot* and spiritual worlds. In Kabbalah, this process is described as follows: 'By fulfilling the commandments and praying, a person "raises the female waters" and apparently unites the *sefirah* of *Malchut* with the *partzuf* of *Zeir Anpin*. In turn, this leads to the "descent of male waters" (*mayin dikhrin*), i.e. the joining of the *partzufim Abba* and *Imma* with the *partzuf Zeir Anpin*.' As a result of this process, the 'sparks of holiness', which have fallen into the lower worlds because of the shattering of the vessels in the world of *Tohu*, are elevated back to their source. Thus, all spiritual worlds and the system of *sefirot* are combined in a single channel, in which the exchange of information takes place unhindered. With the help of this channel, the breakdown in the exchange of communication, which occurred as a result of the sin of Adam, is rectified. Together with the process of elevation of the holy sparks, it realises the process of *tikun* (correction of Creation).

It is important to understand the psychological aspects of the process of elevation. As a consequence of the shattering of the vessels in the world of *Tohu*, new informational entities were formed. They comprised sparks of holiness (information about God) enclosed within the fragments of the vessels (information about self). The informational entities have become the roots for the creation of all the entities with self-awareness, including all that are evil. The defining characteristic of these entities, which arise out of the fragments, is that the awareness of the self dominates the awareness of God. To elevate the sparks we need to reverse this dynamic, and by fulfilling the comandments of the Torah, increase the awareness of God and decrease the awareness of self.

As already mentioned, the negative commandments describe all forms of evil ('Do not kill', 'Do not steal', etc.). In 'The Book of the Intermediates' in the first part of the *Tanya*, the Alter Rebbe explains that some people can conquer evil completely; there are also people who can destroy evil. A person who observes the commandments, laws and statutes destroys evil (transforms darkness into light). Such people are truly righteous and have great influence over the whole of Creation, as well as over many other people. The sages said of such people: 'The righteous uphold the world' [8].

*Chapter 3*

# DIVINE PROVIDENCE

In this chapter, I will attempt to explore the following questions:

1. What is Divine Providence?

2. To whom or what does it apply?

3. How does it work?

4. In what way is it expressed?

First of all, I would like to state a few points.

• According to Kabbalah, evil is an inevitable part of Creation, but the Almighty in His righteousness has given us instruments and rules in order to defeat it.

• With his free will, the human being operates in a world that was created by the Almighty in accordance with His laws, including the law of cause and effect, which is also one of the laws of the Creator.

• The All-powerful Almighty is manifest in everything, including the capacity for self-restraint.

The question of Divine Providence is one that is central to Judaism. Opinion is traditionally divided two ways: the view of Maimonides, and that of the Baal Shem Tov, the founder of the Hasidic movement

## 3.1 THE POSITION OF MAIMONIDES

In *The Guide for the Perplexed*, Maimonides writes that plants and inanimate nature are only viewed by Divine Providence in a general sense. Maimonides also talks about the different levels of Divine Providence among people. He writes: 'Divine Providence applies to each person on the level to which the intellect of that individual has developed. In the case of the illiterate and the unbelieving, Divine Providence relates to them in the same way as it does to animals.' For the purposes of a fuller explanation of this question, Maimonides introduces the gradation of people, too. At the highest level are those people who have a deep understanding of the Torah and natural sciences, and below them are those people who are unbelieving and illiterate. Everyone else is in between. In order to illustrate this grading, Maimonides quotes an example of a city surrounded by a wall (see page 4) [7]. I would propose the following analogy to explain the words of Maimonides:

A man invited three people to visit him. For this purpose, he built a house with ten rooms. Each room was only accessible from the room before it. In the rooms there were tables covered with food. In the first room, the guests were offered the simplest food – bread. In the second, they were offered bread and vegetables. And so on. The tastiest food was in the tenth room. The first room could be entered without any difficulty. In order to enter the second room, it was necessary to complete some kind of task. To move from the second to the third, there was a more difficult task, and so on. The man wanted the guests to try the food he had prepared. He knew which room each person was capable of reaching.

When the first guest arrived, the host knew that he would be able to reach the fourth room, and the man did just that. The host was pleased. The second guest was capable of reaching the seventh room. The host was certain of this, but the man was satisfied when he reached the fifth room and did not go any further. The host was upset. The third guest had the capability to reach the eighth room. However, something strange happened. After tasting the food in that room, the guest did not stop, but attempted to proceed further – into the ninth room. The host helped him.

The host is the Almighty, and the guests are all of us, striving to achieve spiritual enlightenment. Maimonides' view can be confirmed by recalling the words from *Tehillim*: 'My eyes are always to God for He will take my feet out of the net' (*Tehillim*, 25:15). 'Behold the eye of the Lord is to those who fear Him, to those who hope for His kindness' (*Tehillim*, 33:18).

## 3.2 THE POSITION OF THE BAAL SHEM TOV

According to the view of the Baal Shem Tov, Divine Providence controls the actions of all of God's creations, being the life energy of each one and supporting their existence. Moreover, each movement of any entity is connected with all of Creation as a whole. Even the gentle movement of grass is carrying out Divine Providence for all of Creation as a whole. The son of the Alter Rebbe, the Mitteler Rebbe, reconciled the views of Maimonides and the Baal Shem Tov. He introduced the concept of open or 'intimate' Providence (*Hashgacha pnimit*). In this case, Providence acts openly and without disguise. This is the type of Providence that, according to Maimonides, depends on a person's intellect and faith. This form of Providence does not apply to inanimate matter, plants, animals and sinners. The second form of providence, as noted by the Mitteler Rebbe, is hidden or 'external' Providence (*Hashgacha chitzonit*). This providence, which is disguised in the laws of nature, is that of which the Baal Shem Tov spoke.

Before drawing conclusions from the above, let us move over to the world of science for a moment.

## 3.3 CREATION – A SINGLE WHOLE

In his book *What We Cannot Know*, Marcus du Sautoy[44] talks about Oscar II, King of Sweden and Norway, who in 1889, on his sixtieth birthday, offered a prize for solving a mathematical problem. The king put a few questions to the participants in this special lottery. One question was: 'Is the solar system stable, or could it be destroyed at some point in the future?' Among the competitors was a French mathematician called Henri Poincaré. He believed he was sufficiently capable and could win the prize. Poincaré made all the necessary calculations, presented his work, and did indeed receive the prize. Afterwards, something unprecedented happened. Poincaré's work was being prepared for publication in the journal of the Swedish Royal Academy of Sciences, *Acta mathematica*. One of the editors unexpectedly asked the author a question about his calculations. In response, Pointcaré voiced his suggestion that a small change in the position of the planets and the rounding of figures would only

---

44 Marcus du Sautoy (born 1965, London) – a British mathematician, and professor of mathematics at Oxford University. His academic work is mainly connected with group theory and number theory. He plays an active part in the popularisation of science.

express a small change in the predicted orbits. This seemed quite acceptable. However, when he began checking his own calculations, Poincaré discovered that the small margin of error that he had allowed for the planets' starting positions led to a large difference in their orbits [15]. Having attempted to correct his mistake, Poincaré actually established one of the most important mathematical theories of the 20th century – chaos theory. In this case, the insignificant, negligibly small differences (inconsistencies) in the original state of the system led to large differences in its state during the process of evolution. This discovery actually set the limits of human knowledge. Chaos theory was later developed by Edward Lorenz[45] in the mid-20th century. While solving a physics equation in which the original differences were shown four places after the decimal point, Lorenz discovered that their results differed significantly from each other and could develop into two different states. Any minuscule error in observing the original state made it impossible to predict the system's state in the future. Today, Lorenz's discovery is described using the well-known saying that a butterfly fluttering its wings in Brazil can cause a hurricane in Texas.

In his book *Serious Talk: Science and Religion in Dialogue*,[46] quantum physicist and priest John Polkinghorne[47] notes that chaos theory shows us one of the possible mechanisms of action for Divine Providence.

Chaos theory also seriously limits our knowledge of the past and the ability to calculate the states of systems in the past, knowing the current status quo. In the chapter 'Creation', I wrote about the fractal structure of the tree of *sefirot*. As du Sautoy noted, fractals are the geometric signature[48] of chaotic systems.

So, is Creation a single whole or just a sum of its parts? The phenomenon of quantum entanglement (see 'Introduction') provides an answer. In his book *The Outer Limits of Reason* Noson S. Yanofsky writes: 'Entanglement shows that there are no closed systems. Every part of a system can be entangled with other parts outside of the system. All different systems are

45  Edward Norton Lorenz (1917–2008) – an American mathematician and meteorologist, and one of the founders of chaos theory. He was a member of the American Academy of Arts and Sciences, the American Meteorological Society and the US National Academy of Sciences.

46  *Serious Talk: Science and Religion in Dialogue* – John Polkinghorne, Trinity Press International, 1995

47  John Polkinghorne KBE FRS (born 1930, England) – theoretical physicist and Anglican priest, he was professor of mathematical physics at the University of Cambridge.

48  In a chaotic system, a fractal structure is often present. – *Author's note.*

interconnected and the whole universe is one system. One cannot under-stand a system without looking at the whole universe. That is, "the whole is more than just the sum of its parts".'

It can be added that not only the universe is a single whole. Creation is a single whole. Slight movements of an electron on the fringe of the universe affect the taste of tea in my cup. Note the position of Baal Shem Tov.

## 3.4 MIRACLES IN THE TORAH

The purpose of this chapter is not to explain miracles, but to attempt to comprehend what a miracle is and understand some of the principles by which the Almighty governs our world. Before proceeding further, though, let us ask a question: Do we have the right to attempt to comprehend the actions of the Almighty? Are we not trespassing in a forbidden place? After all, speaking through the prophet Yeshayahu, the Almighty said: 'For My thoughts are not your thoughts, neither are your ways My ways.'

Maimonides provides an answer to this question in *The Guide for the Perplexed*, as he comments on Moses' words addressed to the Almighty: 'And now, if I have indeed found favour in Your eyes, pray let me know Your ways, so that I may know You, so that I may find favour in Your eyes...' (*Shemot*, 33:13). Maimonides states that two conclusions can be drawn from these words from the Torah:

1. The Almighty can be recognised by His ways.

2. By knowing the ways of the Almighty, Moses knows the Almighty Himself.

Maimonides draws a further conclusion from this extract: One who knows God finds favour in His eyes. He writes: 'Not one who simply fasts and prays, but one who possesses knowledge of God finds favour in His eyes. The benevolence and the wrath of the Almighty, His nearness and distance correspond to a person's level of knowledge' [7].

Nachmanides and other commentators have written that the Almighty created our world so that, having broken free from the veil of material things, mankind might come to know his Creator.

WHAT IS A MIRACLE?

The most widespread definition of a miracle found in both Jewish and universal sources is this: A miracle is an event or phenomenon that contravenes the laws of nature.

This definition contains an error. If we suppose that the laws of nature have been broken, then this means that we know and understand them.

In reality, only a tiny part of the existing laws of nature have been studied by humanity, and we do not know the full extent of even those laws that we consider to be understood.

**Rather, it is the creation of our world by the Almighty, and the granting of the law that governs it, that should be considered a miracle.**

This is a law, not laws. I suggest that all the laws of nature that we observe are the consequence of a single law that the Almighty granted to our world, and which was hidden from us by a thick veil. Let us attempt to explain this.

In the *Tanya*, in the section called 'The Gateway of Unity and Belief', Alter Rebbe writes: 'Thus the unfathomable creations of heaven and earth are manifest. However, their eyes are blind and unable to see the vast difference between the actions and creation of mankind who creates out of what already exists, only changing the form and image, such as transforming a piece of silver into a vessel, and the creation of heaven and earth out of nothing. **This is a much greater miracle** than, for example, the parting of the waters of the Red Sea when the Almighty caused the sea to move back under the force of a strong easterly wind that blew all night, so that the waters parted and formed a wall. If the Almighty had stopped the wind for a minute, the waters would have collapsed again, as their nature intended, and, of course, the walls would have ceased to stand, even though this property of water was also created out of nothing and was constantly renewed' [8].

As Maimonides points out, one of the main characteristics of the Almighty is the absence of plurality within Him – His oneness. The Almighty created our world by emitting a single ray of Divine Light. This single ray of light cannot carry plurality – it carries oneness. Let us also note that the Almighty is the only cause of our world and its single form.

Modern science is beginning to move towards the understanding that the world is governed by a single law. Einstein's equation $E = mc^2$ brought mass and energy together into a single whole. Einstein's theory of general relativity united space and time in a single whole.

Physicists have now demonstrated that the four forces known to us (gravity, electromagnetism, strong nuclear force and weak nuclear force) represented a single force at the moment of the Big Bang (Creation). This question arises: Is it possible to know the single law of the Almighty?

Forty-nine gates of wisdom were opened to our teacher Moses. Nachmanides believes that the fiftieth gate of the knowledge of the Creator Himself was not opened to Moses. Commenting on an extract from the Torah: 'Man shall not see Me and live', the Maharal of Prague (1525–1609) wrote: 'At the fiftieth level, comes the understanding of the unity of all things.' From this, it is possible to suppose that we are not meant to understand the single law.

The sages of the Talmud based their definition of miracles on a phrase from *Kohelet*: 'What has been is what will be, and what has been done is what will be done, and there is nothing new under the sun' (*Kohelet*, 1:9), stating that the Almighty granted the law to Creation, having already placed inside it the ability to perform miracles. Thus, for example, when the sea was created, it was ordered to part at a particular moment. In his commentary on *Kohelet*, Saadia Gaon writes about the planning of miracles at the time of Creation. In *The Guide for the Perplexed*, Maimonides also states, based on the above extract from *Kohelet*, that all miracles were planned when the world was created.

From a scientific point of view, it is possible to assume that a law granted at the time of the creation of the world can contain the ability to dynamically manage a set of states for any system.

In his treatise 'On the resurrection of mortals', Maimonides divides miracles into two categories: possible and impossible. In Maimonides' view, possible miracles, such as the plague of locusts in Egypt, occur in accordance with the laws of our world. On the other hand, he counts miracles that cannot be explained by the laws of nature as impossible.

However, it is not possible to completely agree with this.

What would Maimonides, who was a doctor, have said upon seeing a dead person being raised back to life? Doubtless he would have called it unreal, and a miraculous phenomenon. Today, though, bringing a clinically dead person back to life happens reasonably frequently and it can be explained by the laws of nature.

Hence, it follows that all phenomena that are considered to be miracles occur in accordance with the law that the Almighty gave to the world during Creation. As science develops, we are beginning to increasingly understand the law of the Almighty, although we will never know it completely.

Judging from the above information, it is possible to draw the following preliminary conclusions:

• We do not know all the laws of nature.

• We do not understand the essence of the laws of nature that we already know.

• The ultimate miracle is the Creation of our world by the Almighty and the granting of a single law by means of which the Almighty governs absolutely.

• The single law, which the Almighty gave to our world at the moment of Creation, has not changed since that time.

**This law contains all the possible variants of the states of any system, including miraculous circumstances. It includes the ability to control and manage the state of all our world's systems without pressure, violence, and the severing of cause-effect relationships.**

The last conclusion requires some explanation. Nachmanides writes: 'Thus, out of full and absolute nothing, He extracted the subtlest foundation which had no material nature, created energy, and was ready to assume a form and transfer from a potential state into action, and this is the primary material, which the Greeks called *ayuli*. However, after *ayuli* He created nothing, but only formed and made, since from it He derived all things, clothed them in different forms, and transformed them.'

In Rabbi Judah Halevi's book (*Sefer ha-Kuzari*) it says: 'According to nature, life follows its own course, but, from the point of view of the Torah, the usual order can change. Harmony between these is when the usual order only changes in accordance with that which is in its nature, since these changes are due to the original will of the Almighty and were prepared during the six days of Creation' [6].

In *Kohelet* it says: '…Everything that God made, that will be forever; we cannot add to it, nor can we subtract from it…' (*Kohelet,* 3:14).

MIRACLES AND EXTRA LOW PROBABILITY PHENOMENA

As has already been mentioned, all phenomena in our world can be called miracles, since they are the consequence of the single law of the Almighty, which he gave to our world. However, a few phenomena are highlighted in our perception – generally those that occur extremely rarely. For example, if a monkey sits at a piano and happens to play a work by Bach, we would perceive this as a miracle. We would call it a miracle if a thousand slot machines all came up with the same combination at the same time. The phenomena described above do not contradict the laws of nature, but they are highly improbable. The likelihood of their occurring is an infinitesimal quantity above zero.

From a scientific point of view, this provided the basis for interpreting a miracle as an extremely improbable phenomenon in our world. The seventh Lubavitcher Rebbe objected to this explanation. He wrote: 'From the point of view of modern science, no one can say that the miracles written in the Torah are impossible. However, it is also categorically forbidden to reduce miracles to phenomena whose uniqueness lies in their low probability.'

At this point, an apparent contradiction arises. On one hand, the Rebbe agrees with the notion that, from the scientific point of view, miracles are extremely improbable phenomena. However, at the same time, he categorically objects to miracles being identified as such. Let us attempt to explain. A miracle is indeed a unique occurrence, since it happens extremely rarely. However, a miracle's uniqueness is in the way it manifests in the right place at the right time. An explanation of this will be given at the end of this section.

So, is the world probabilistic? It seems to me that the probabilistic nature of the world is a kind of curtain separating us from the truth of a greater reality or realities. As Einstein said, 'God does not play dice with the universe.' The Almighty, who is beyond time, possesses absolute knowledge.

**Hence, we can conclude that probability does not exist for the Almighty. All possible states of systems exist before Him, and He can choose any of them with 100 per cent certainty, according to His desire. For the Almighty, probability does not exist as an objective reality, i.e. one that does not depend on Him. That which seems objective to us, given our position as local observers, does not appear that way to Him.**

Let us explain the above with a few examples from the Torah.

• The miracle of the parting of the sea
In the Torah it is written: '…And the Lord led the sea with the strong east wind all night, and He made the sea into dry land…' (*Shemot*, 14:21). An enormously powerful gust of wind does not contravene the laws of nature, although the fact that the gust of wind had just the right amount of power needed to part the sea, and that it blew in the right direction, at the right time, in the right place, yet did not affect the Jews standing on the shore, seems a highly improbable occurrence. **For the Almighty, though, probability does not exist.**

• The miracle of manna

Since the manna was edible, it was presumably an organic substance. Edible organic substances usually consist of carbon, hydrogen, nitrogen and oxygen. All these elements are present in the Earth's atmosphere. The laws of physics do not rule out the spontaneous combining of these elements in the Earth's atmosphere, but such an event is extremely improbable. **For the Almighty, though, probability does not exist.**

• The miracle of Korah being swallowed by the earth

The laws of physics do not rule out cracks appearing in the ground. They occur, for example, during earthquakes. However, the fact that the earth opened up at the right moment in time, in the right place, and swallowed up particular people is an extremely improbable occurrence. **For the Almighty, though, probability does not exist.**

### MIRACLE AND INTELLECT

It was mentioned earlier that the law given to the world by the Almighty never changes. This point of view can be explained and expanded upon. First, though, I would like to remind the reader of the main points in the discussion on miracles that have taken place in Judaism.

**First.** According to the opinion of several Talmud sages, as well as a host of Jewish philosophers (Saadia Gaon, Maimonides, et al.), the Almighty included the need for the occurrence of miracles in the law that He gave to our world at the moment of Creation, so the miracles were planned. In other words, the creation of miracles requires no further intervention from the Almighty.

This point of view can be borne out by the following argument. The Almighty is absolute perfection. He knows that His work is perfect, and achieves the necessary results with minimal effort. If, when performing a miracle, the Almighty changed His own law every time, then the principle of minimal intervention would be lost.

Below, we will explain the question of the intervention or non-intervention of the Almighty during the miracle process.

**Second.** According to the viewpoint of Nachmanides and the Baal Shem Tov, the founder of Hasidism, the Almighty intervenes in the world order, meaning He changes the laws of nature that He established, and then miracles take place.

The contradiction can be resolved as follows. The law, which was given to our world by the Almighty during Creation, never changes, but it can be manifest in two modes.

**Let us call the first mode the planned one. This means that the law given during Creation is applied with no active intervention from Divine or human intellect.**

**The second mode is that of active submission to the intellect, whereby the law remains as before, i.e. given to Creation in the beginning, but it is influenced by human or Divine intellect.**

Let us explain this with an example. During Creation, the Almighty gave the world a law that functioned according to plan and consequently formed protons, neutrons, atoms, molecules, stars and galaxies. This continued until a structure appeared that possessed intellect – mankind. Let us look at an example. The seventh Lubavitcher Rebbe said that when the previous Rebbe was a boy, he went for a walk with his father. While walking, he pulled a leaf off a tree. His father reproached him, saying that, by pulling off a leaf, he had altered the course of the whole of Creation. What exactly had happened? According to the first way in which the law is manifest, the leaf should have stayed on the tree until autumn and then fallen of its own accord. However, the boy's intellect had given a command to his brain which, in turn, gave a command to his hand, which then pulled off the leaf. Thus, the boy transferred the law to the second mode – active submission to the intellect. **I would like to note that, despite the change in the way the law is manifest, the law itself remained unchanged. The force of gravity remained the force of gravity, electromagnetism remained electromagnetism, etc.** The right to change the mode in which the law is manifest with the help of our intellect, which was granted to us by the Almighty, is our likeness to Him. However, our intellect affects the law in a limited way, whereas that of the Almighty affects it in an absolute way.

In *The Book of the Wars of the Lord*, Rabbi Levi ben Gershon (Ralbag) writes that only the human intellect can change the course of chance (natural) events.

The following example can illustrate this view. Imagine that a group of people are inside a huge palace. There are many rooms, and there is food and drink in each of these. The people are given rules for how to live. However, there is one condition: in the centre of the palace there is a screen. Once a day, a number appears on the screen, consisting of fifty randomly selected digits. The people are told that they can leave the palace when a number made up of only ones appears on the screen. They all understand that the probability of this happening is close to zero. The screen is linked to a computer located in a separate room that the people cannot access. A certain someone works in that room. He has programmed the computer to generate a number consisting of fifty digits once a day. That someone does not intervene in the computer's work. He only supports it to ensure it functions. However, the people do not know that this person has included two modes in this programme. The first mode is as described above. But there is another one, too. The programmer can press a button, switch off the random selection, and create any fifty-digit number he desires. One fine day, he switches the programme to the second mode and selects a number made up of fifty ones. The people see the number on the screen, realise that a miracle has occurred, and leave the palace.

**CONCLUSIONS**

**First.** During Creation, the Almighty gave the world a law by which it functions. This law consists of particular physical forces that operate in our world, affording it numerous parameters and laws of interaction. This law also determines the intellectual connection between the created entities in our world and the intellect of the Almighty.

**Second.** This law is unchangeable. It contains the potential capability for any phenomena in our world, including the extraordinary or miraculous. However, the concept of probability does not exist for the Almighty, since all possible system states are open to Him, and He can choose any of these with 100 per cent certainty.

**Third.** This law has two modes of operation.
1. The first mode ('natural' – *Elohim*) is when the law works in accordance with the installed programme.
2. The second mode ('supernatural' – *Havayah*) is when the Almighty intervenes and makes the law directly obedient to His intellect. However, we must remember the phrase, 'Thus you should know that *Havayah* is *Elohim*.'

**Fourth.** Miracles occur in our world as a result of God's intervention and His switching the law from the first mode to the second. In this case, the concept of probability loses its meaning, and any extremely rare phenomena, such as those shown above, can become reality.

## 3.5 THE MECHANISM OF DIVINE PROVIDENCE

It is impossible to speak with absolute certainty about the mechanism of Divine Providence. However, there are some suppositions that can be considered.

In the chapter entitled 'A Short Introduction to Kabbalah', I mentioned the concept of higher and lower knowledge, as introduced by Alter Rebbe. Let us remind the reader that higher knowledge is the inherent state of the Almighty – *Ein Sof* (not finite). It encompasses everything, including that which does not exist, as well as that which will be, without discerning between good and evil, and without exerting any direct impact on our world. Lower knowledge relates to the creation of worlds and is to be found in the system of *sefirot*. In my view, this is the active intellect and it is located in the *sefirah* of *Chochma* in the world of *Atzilut*. In the process of the informational exchange (see Chapter 1, 'Creation', page 31), information enters into the higher *sefirah* of *Chochma* in the world of *Atzilut*. The reverse effect occurs through the *sefirah* of *Keter*, which symbolises the Creator's will and desire. As we have already noted, each of the *sefirot* contains the remaining *sefirot*, presenting itself as a fractal. Therefore, apart from the higher *sefirah* of *Chochma* in the world of *Atzilut,* and also the *sefirot* of *Chochma* in the worlds of *Beriah, Yetzirah and Asiyah,* there are countless multitudes of *Chochma* contained within the other *sefirot*. They are all combined and form a kind of 'intellectual' skeleton of the system of spiritual worlds.

**PRAYER**

Daily prayers were ordered by the sages after the destruction of the second Temple, to replace sacrifices. According to the Talmud, prayer can change the course of Divine Providence. Let us examine this more closely.

The Temple was a unique phenomenon on earth. Within it, there was a direct communication channel with higher spiritual worlds. After the destruction of the Temple, people lost the ability to use this channel, so prayer was introduced. However, certain conditions need to be fulfilled for the prayer to be heard and actioned:

1. It must be heard.

2. An information channel must be created for this purpose.

3. This channel should be free from noise and interference.

4. The channel should be used to transmit meaningful information.

A person creates an informational channel as a result of active participation in the informational exchange with spiritual worlds by means of studying the Torah and fulfilling the commandments. The purity of the channel is protected from noise and interference by means of special techniques of prayer (*kavvanah*), which require deep focus and concentration.

If a praying person possesses the required knowledge and fulfils the commandments of the Torah, then during the prayer process the *sefirah* of *Chochma* in his soul is activated, which, in turn, is connected with the *sefirah* of *Chochma* in the higher worlds. In this case, the prayer reaches the highest level.

If a person does not possess the required knowledge and recites the prayer automatically, without understanding its meaning, then only his soul's *midot* will be activated. This prayer does not reach the level of the *sefirah* of *Chochma* in the higher worlds, and is much less effective. The Alter Rebbe wrote about this in his book *Torah Or*, saying that a person who has served the Almighty without knowledge is like an animal, since his service is based on animal instincts [9].

**HOW IS DIVINE PROVIDENCE EXPRESSED?**
This question is extremely complex and does not have a simple answer. Maimonides believed that the reward for our actions is only granted to us in the World to Come. Let us attempt to examine this question in more detail. In life, we usually want good physical and mental health, an absence of suffering and difficulty, financial security, a nice family (with a spouse and children) and self-fulfilment. Let us take a look at these qualities in the examples given to us by the Torah: Noah, Abraham, Isaac, Jacob, Moses, Aaron, David and Solomon.

• Physical health. This is not given to all of them. Isaac was blind, and Jacob's hip was damaged.

• Financial security was not always achievable, either. David was poor for long periods of his life.

• Having a nice family and raising children properly did not work out well for them all. We recall Noah's son, Ham; Abraham's Ishmael; Isaac's Esau; and David's Absalom.

• An absence of suffering and difficulty. None of the above was granted total well-being (everyone was tested).

• Mental health and self-fulfilment are granted to all of them, but at the end of his life, Solomon went off the righteous path and became an idol worshipper. The Lord truly works in mysterious ways! It is not for mankind to fathom the ways of Divine Providence, so we must do as the Almighty has told us and hope for the best.

## DIVINE RADAR
In modern science, there is a concept of mental space. A person's mental space has an infinite number of dimensions. It would be absurd to suggest that it is closed. On the other hand, it is clearly vertically connected with all the spiritual worlds and has its own prototype there. Through these higher worlds, it is connected with the mental space of other people. Every material entity in our world has its own informational prototype in higher worlds.

The influence of the Almighty on the informational prototypes of the mental space of all entities in higher worlds could be the mechanism of Divine Providence. This influence can be illustrated by the following simple example. If you imagine lower knowledge as a radar, then, as a result of the participation of a person or other entities in the informational process, there is a 'spot' on the radar that corresponds to each mental space. The greater the level of participation, the greater the attention the Almighty pays it. However, it is important to understand that we must all increase our participation in the informational process, although our increasing 'spot' on the radar will attract not only increased attention but also increased responsibility.

## FORMS OF DIVINE PROVIDENCE
Let us ask the question: 'Which forms does Divine Providence take?'

• The Almighty gave our world a physical law, as expressed in the action of four forces (gravitation, electromagnetism, and strong and weak nuclear force). This law never changes. In the 1920s the great German female mathematician Amalie Emmy Noether demonstrated that the law of conservation of energy is a consequence of the immutability of the laws of physics in time. Thus, a law does not change, but needs constant confirmation. This is the Kabbalistic concept of the continuous nature of the process of creation. The Almighty continuously renews all of Creation, thus confirming the law and enabling the manifestation of all entities and worlds. (See Chapter 1, Creation, page 39.). The way the law is applied could be changed by God influencing human intellect.

• The Almighty realises His providence by openly governing human intellect. For example, when Abimelech, the king of the Philistines, took Abraham's wife Sarah into his palace, 'God said to him [Abimelech] in a dream "And now, return the man's wife, because he is a prophet, and he will pray for you and [you will] live; but if you do not return [her], know that you will surely die"' (*Bereishit*, 20:7). When Laban the Aramean overtook our forefather Jacob on the way to the Holy Land, God came to Laban in a dream at night, and warned him not to say anything to Jacob, either good or evil.

• The Almighty can exercise His providence by the hidden governing of human intellect – for example, in the book of Exodus, when the Almighty said to Moses: 'But I will harden Pharaoh's heart, and I will increase My signs and My wonders in the land of Egypt' (*Shemot*, 7:3). In this case, God secretly limited Pharaoh's freedom of choice, thus exercising His providence.

• The Almighty exercises His providence by giving human intellect the right, through speech and actions, to change the way in which the law works, to a limited extent.

*Chapter 4*

# KABBALAH AND QUANTUM PHYSICS

## 4.1 THE ORIGIN AND MAIN IDEAS OF QUANTUM PHYSICS

In 1900, Max Planck[49] solved the problem of the so-called ultraviolet catastrophe. To explain what this means, according to classical physics equations, the radiation of an ideal black body should increase ad infinitum, but this did not happen. Planck supposed that the radiation from the black body was emitted in packets (quanta) proportionate to the frequency of the radiation, and thus the problem was solved. A few years later, Albert Einstein used this discovery to explain the photoelectric effect, for which he was awarded the Nobel Prize. In 1911, as a result of some brilliantly conducted experiments, Ernest Rutherford[50] discovered the structure of the atom in which the positively charged nucleus is surrounded by negatively charged electrons. However, there was still a problem. According to classical electrodynamics equations, the electrons rotating around the positive nucleus should have constantly radiated energy and ultimately been swallowed up by the nucleus, but in fact this did not happen. In 1913, the

---

49  Max Planck (1858–1947) – a German theoretical physicist and a founder of quantum physics. He was a laureate of the Nobel Prize in Physics, and other awards, and a member of the Prussian Academy of Sciences as well as many foreign scientific societies and academies of science.

50  Ernest Rutherford (1871–1937) – a New Zealand-born British physicist. He is known as the 'father' of nuclear physics. He won the Nobel Prize in Chemistry in 1908. In 1911, by means of his famous experiment with the scattering of alpha particles, he proved the existence of the positively charged nucleus in atoms, and negatively charged electrons around it. Based on the results of this experiment, he developed the planetary model of the atom.

physicist Niels Bohr developed a mathematical model of the atom that supported Rutherford's model.

This was based on the following two tenets:

1. Electrons can occupy only certain discrete orbits.

2. Radiation energy swallowed up or emitted by the electron determines the difference between the two stationary states and is equivalent to the frequency multiplied by Planck's constant [16]. Bohr's model raised many questions. It determined only certain orbits available to electrons. The location of an electron while moving from one orbit to another remained unclear. Rutherford, to whom Bohr presented his model, commented that, while moving from a higher orbit to a lower one, an electron radiates a strictly defined packet of energy proportional to the frequency, and thus it must 'know' in advance which orbit it is going to move to.

Today, quantum physics, along with Einstein's theory of general relativity, is the most comprehensive theory that describes our reality. The predictions of quantum physics are almost always borne out by experiments. The behaviour of quantum entities differs significantly from that which is familiar to us in classical physics. While a completely accurate value can be given for a variable for any object in classical physics, quantum physics relies only on probability. The evolution of a quantum system is described with the help of Schrödinger's[51] wave function, which takes into account the probability of certain variables. Quantum entities can behave both as waves and as particles. Their behaviour depends on the conditions of the experiment. Heisenberg's uncertainty principle[52] imposes restrictions on the possible simultaneous measurement of the position and impulse of particles.

---

51  Erwin Schrödinger (1887–1961) – an Austrian theoretical physicist, and one of the founders of quantum mechanics. He was a member of many academies of science around the world, including a foreign member of the USSR Academy of Sciences. Schrödinger achieved many fundamental results in the field of quantum theory, which formed the basis of wave mechanics.

52  Werner Karl Heisenberg (1901–1976) – a German theoretical physicist, one of the founders of quantum mechanics, laureate of the Nobel Prize in Physics (1932), member of many academies and scientific societies around the world. Heisenberg is the author of a range of fundamental results in quantum physics, in particular the uncertainty principle.

Despite the fact that quantum theory is confirmed by experiment, many questions are still left unanswered:

• Is the mathematical formalism of quantum mechanics the description of reality, or merely a convenient means of calculating the parameters of a system?

• The problem of measurement. In the process of contact between a quantum entity and a classical measuring device, why does an abrupt transition take place from the state of superposition (which can be described using Schrödinger's wave function) to a classical state in which the device determines a completely concrete value for the measured quantity?

• Why do macro-objects, which consist of quantum entities, behave in a classical way?

• In the introduction to quantum physics a question was asked: how does a photon 'know' what the experimenter is going to do?

The answers to these questions have given rise to the so-called interpretations. However, before moving on to a description of the main interpretations, let us consider the question of probability. The ideas of the scientific community regarding probability can in general be divided into two groups, as accepted by modern science: 1) probability is an inseparable property of reality; 2) probability is a subjective property, a degree of the assessment of reality, or the degree of our ignorance.

The second (subjective) approach towards probability was developed by the English mathematician and priest Thomas Bayes, in the 18th century. With a few simplifications, his theory can be illustrated with the following example. When we look out of the window in the morning and see the sun and a clear sky, we estimate the probability of rain to be 5 per cent. In the middle of the day, seeing the sky covered with clouds, we change our opinion and estimate the probability of rain to now be 75 per cent. In this example, the suggested probabilities are our own personal opinion, and bear no relation to actual reality.

Albert Einstein believed the probabilistic nature of quantum mechanics to be a sign of its incompleteness. Hence the famous phrase, 'God does not play dice.'

However, let us return to the interpretations. There are rather a lot of them at the present time. Instead of overwhelming the reader, let us introduce the main ones.

• The Copenhagen interpretation was proposed by Niels Bohr[53] and Werner Heisenberg. In the opinion of these scientists, Schrödinger's wave function was mathematical formalism, and did not describe the properties of reality; it is impossible and pointless to speak about the properties of a quantum entity without taking into account interaction with measuring equipment ('measurement makes reality'); as a result of interaction with measuring apparatus, a quantum system shifts abruptly to a classical state (the collapse of wave function); classical description is the only language of knowledge available to us; the principle of complementarity states that quantum entities possess the properties of both waves and particles, which manifest themselves depending on the conditions of the experiment.

• Interpretation of the relative state (the state of many-worlds). This interpretation was proposed by the scientist Hugh Everett in 1957 and developed further by Bryce DeWitt.[54] The main points are: Schrödinger's wave function is a description of reality; during the process of measurement the formation of a new system takes place: quantum entity – measuring apparatus – an observer who finds his own wave function; in turn, this system is connected with its environment (thus Everett arrives at the concept of universal wave function); during the process of measurement, all possible results are realised, although the results are hereby spread across a multitude of worlds, and each possible result corresponds to one of them. We can observe one value of the measurable variable, since we are in one of the many worlds [26].

• The Interpretation of von Neumann-Wigner. In his book *Mathematical*

---

53  Niels Bohr (1885–1962) – a Danish theoretical physicist and public figure. One of the founders of modern physics. Laureate of the Nobel Prize in Physics (1922). Member of the Danish Royal Society, and its president from 1939. He was a member of over 20 academies of science around the world, including a foreign honorary member of the USSR Academy of Sciences. Bohr is known as the founder of the first quantum atomic theory, and an active participant in the fundamental development of quantum mechanics. He also made a significant contribution to the development of the theory of the atomic nucleus and nuclear reactions.

54  Bryce DeWitt (1923–2004) – an American theoretical physicist, member of the American National Academy of Sciences and the American Academy of Arts and Sciences.

*Foundations of Quantum Mechanics*, John von Neumann[55] states that, according to the laws of quantum mechanics, the collapse of wave function can occur at any point in the causal chain – from measuring equipment to the subjective perception of the observer. This interpretation is basically formulated as follows: the laws of quantum mechanics are correct, but they only describe one system – the material world. There are external observers who cannot be described by the laws of quantum mechanics, i.e. the human (animate) intellect, which captures measurements in the brain, causing wave function to collapse.

• QBism – this interpretation is an approach based on the ideas developed by Thomas Bayes. The main points are: wave function does not describe reality, but is an instruction for the observer to evaluate the state of the quantum system; measuring apparatus is the continuation of the observer's mind; the collapse of wave function occurs in the observer's consciousness; all probabilities calculated according to Schrödinger's equation are subjective [19].

• Decoherence. Decoherence is known as the informational exchange between a system and its environment. This exchange takes place during the process of measurement, and we receive information that we did not previously have. This process is irreversible. According to the theory of decoherence, the appearance of a system on a classical level takes place as a consequence of the exchange of information with classical measuring apparatus. Also, according to the theory of decoherence, macro-objects made up of quantum particles appear as classical when they participate in a continuous informational exchange with the environment.

• The relational interpretation proposed by the Italian physicist Carlo Rovelli. The main points are: during the process of measurement, it is not the 'objective properties of the system' that are determined, but the result of the system's interaction with the measuring apparatus. Therefore, the objective properties of the system are not available to us.

---

55 John von Neumann (1903–1957) – a Jewish-born American mathematician who made an important contribution to quantum physics, quantum logic, functional analysis, set theory, computing, economics and other branches of science. He is most well known as the person whose name is associated wth the architecture of most modern computers (the so-called von Neumann architecture).

There are also many other interpretations, but we will not examine them in this book.

In my opinion, the main shortcoming of the above interpretations is the fact that they examine Creation without considering the Creator.

## 4.2 QUANTUM ENTANGLEMENT AND KABBALAH

The essence of quantum entanglement (see page 28) is explained by the example of two particles which, after interacting, move apart by a distance up to universal proportions. Then, measurement of the properties of one of them (for example, spin – the angular momentum of elementary particles) determines the outcome of the measurements of the properties of a second particle. There is a full correlation between the two sets of results. This fact has now been confirmed by a multitude of experiments.

The reader may ask: 'What does this have to do with Kabbalah?'

However, strange as it may seem, it is in the works of the early Kabbalists that we find ideas and viewpoints that point towards the principle of quantum entanglement. One of the founders of Kabbalah, Rabbi Abraham ben David, put forward an interesting notion. He maintained that the Divine attributes of *Chesed* and *Gevurah* were a single whole before they were separated in order to enable their interaction in the future [3].

## 4.3 QUANTUM PHYSICS FROM A KABBALISTIC PERSPECTIVE

I believe that we have no reason to suppose that, in the chain of human-animal-plant-electron, the mental component completely disappears. In the chapter entitled 'Creation', I suggest that the mental and material components of our world consist of information that is presented to us in different forms. Arizal taught that, even in inanimate matter, such as the stones and the earth, a soul and a spiritual life force is present. It occurs as a consequence of the embodiment within the inanimate object of letters deriving from the ten utterances of the Almighty, by means of which the world was created – i.e. out of information. These letters (information), according to Arizal, carry life forces and existence even to inanimate matter, allowing it to be manifest as existence out of non-existence [10]. Therefore, Kabbalah presents a standpoint that philosophy terms 'neutral monism'.

The notion in science and philosophy that accepts the general spirituality of nature is called panpsychism. The idea of panpsychism is found in ancient

Greek philosophy, as well as in the teachings of Gottfried Wilhelm Leibniz[56], Arthur Schopenhauer[57] and Carl Jung[58].

I would like to present the following system of postulates for the reader to judge.

1. Creation is a hierarchical system of informational worlds with a measuring rod (see 'Introduction to Kabbalah') at the 'entrance' to every world.

2. This system is supported by uninterrupted information exchange from 'top' to 'bottom' and vice versa.

3. Every elementary particle of our world is an informational system with a fixed behavioural program that can be changed only by the Creator.

4. Thus they are analogous to the notion of angels (in his book 'Guide of Perplexed' Maimonides called all the forces of nature 'angels').

5. Each informational entity of our world has informational prototypes in each of the informational worlds and interacts with them.

6. Any interaction of the informational entities of our world is accompanied by the interaction of their informational prototypes in higher worlds.

7. In the process of experimentation (for example, in the 'quantum eraser' experiment) informational prototypes of photons, measuring devices and the consciousness of the experimenters interact.

---

56  Gottfried Wilhelm Leibniz (1646–1716) – a German philosopher, logician, mathematician, mechanician, physicist, lawyer, historian, diplomat, inventor and linguist. He was the founder and the first president of the Berlin Academy of Sciences, and foreign member of the French Academy of Sciences.

57  Arthur Schopenhauer (1788–1860) – a German philosopher. He was one of the most famous thinkers of irrationalism, tended towards German romanticism, was interested in mysticism, regarded the principal works of Immanuel Kant very highly, and valued the philosophical ideas of Buddhism. He criticised his contemporaries Hegel and Fichte. He called the existing world 'the worst of all possible worlds', for which he acquired the nickname 'the philosopher of pessimism'. His main philosophical work was *The World as Will and Representation*, and Schopenhauer worked at commentating and popularising this until his death.

58  Carl Gustav Jung (1875–1961) – a Swiss psychiatrist and founder of analytical psychology.

8. As a result, the photon 'knows' and acts according to its inbuilt program.

9. Since the concepts of distance and location are absent in the higher worlds, informational entities determine each other only due to their interaction, which projects into only one 'classical' outcome in our world.

10. Human soul (consciousness as a part of the soul) is a unique informational entity in Creation since it possesses the power of self-learning and self-awareness. In the chapter 'Miracles in the Torah' it was shown that human intelligence can alter the course of natural events.

There are traditional objections to the role of human consciousness.

1. What if the results of the experiment were recorded by a computer?

2. Can animal consciousness achieve the same effect?

The possible answers are as follows. It does not matter whether the experimenter is present; the key point is that the setup of the experiment was organised by a human being. Animals cannot stage any kind of experiment.

With regard to quantum entanglement, it can only occur if particles have interacted in the past. The correlation between Divine attributes can also only be observed if they were previously a single whole.

The following hypothesis can be put forward to explain this. While examining the interaction of particles in our world, Asiyah, we must take into account the existence of other informational worlds. Every informational entity of our world has its prototype (root) in spiritual worlds. It is perfectly acceptable that, during the interaction of particles in our world, their roots in spiritual worlds merge and are transformed into a single whole. Later, communications between these particles, regardless of the distance between them, are realised through their mutual root. There is of course no scientific proof of this sort of interaction, but here I am espousing the position of Kabbalah.

From my point of view, the interpretations most similar to the one given above are those of decoherence, von Neyman—Wigner and QBism.

The reader must remember though that none of the existing interpretations of quantum mechanics is currently supported by evidence.

*Chapter 5*

# THE SOUL AND INFORMATION

In Judaism, there is no single simple description of the soul, the interaction between body and soul, and the fate of the soul after death, as well as concepts such as paradise (*Gan Eden*), hell (*Gehenna*), the resurrection of the dead, and the World to Come. In the scripture of the Torah, these questions are almost never directly addressed, and although we can find the main points in the books of the prophets, the information they contain is generally brief and fragmented.

The soul is first mentioned in the book of *Bereishit*: 'And the Lord God formed man of dust from the ground, and He breathed into his nostrils the soul of life, and man became a living soul' (*Bereishit,* 2:7). It is already clear from this verse that the main property of the soul is that it gives life to the body. In *The Guide for the Perplexed*, Maimonides writes that the first man possessed intellect, thus the Almighty gave him the task of naming all the animals according to their characteristics. Hence, we can conclude that the soul also possesses intellectual qualities. We will continue to analyse this concept below.

## 5.1 THE SOUL IN ANCIENT GREEK PHILOSOPHY

In the poems of Homer, the soul is defined as an entity that leaves the body at the moment of death. After this, the soul descends into the underworld, where it exists in the form of the shadow of the deceased person. The presence of a soul, according to Homer, distinguishes a living human body from a non-living one. Homer does not attribute any other characteristics to the soul [21].

Thales, a pre-Socratic Greek philosopher, believed that everything that moves has a soul, even magnets. In the late fifth century BC, Greek philosophy began to attribute other properties to the soul, such as pleasure, sexual desire, bravery and sorrow. Pythagoras and Empedocles, also pre-Socratic Greek philosophers, believed that plants have a soul. They also introduced the concept of reincarnation. Heraclitus, in his works, wrote that the soul possesses wisdom.

The soul is one of the central themes of Plato's philosophy. Let us pause to consider just the main milestones in the teaching of this philosopher, as it would be impossible to include it in full in this book, due to the vast amount of material.

• The soul is responsible for all of a person's mental and psychological activity.

• The human soul consists of three parts: appetite, spirit and reason.

• The soul possesses intellectual capabilities.

• The soul is an immortal entity, and nothing can destroy it.

• After death, the soul retains its intellectual qualities, having acquired them during life.

• The nature of the soul and the body is different. (Here, Plato adopts the standpoint of dualism.)

In Aristotle's philosophy, the relationship between soul and body is like the relationship between form and matter. Aristotle believed that plants, animals and humans have a soul. He presented the soul as a system of active capabilities, carrying out the body's vital functions. Agreeing with Plato that the soul has no material nature, Aristotle believed the soul capable of existing only in conjunction with the body, and thus it was deprived of all capabilities after death.

## 5.2 PRE-KABBALIST VIEWS

A more comprehensive presentation of the pre-Kabbalist view on the soul is given in the book by Saadia Gaon, *The Book of Beliefs and Opinions*. Saadia

Gaon believes the soul to be a created entity that comes down to our world in order to carry out certain functions. According to his view, the soul is divided into several parts or levels.

*Nefesh* (the vitalising soul) is responsible for carrying out the body's vital functions; *ruach* (spirit) is responsible for emotions; *neshama* (soul) is responsible for the intellectual functions; *chaya* (life) is responsible for the highest level of intellectual ability; and *yechida* (uniqueness) embodies the particle of God in a person's soul. In Kabbalah, *nefesh* corresponds to *Malchut*, *ruah* to *midot*, *neshama* to *Binah*, *chaya* to *Chochma* and *yehida* to *Keter*.

Saadia Gaon does not accept that there are several souls in a person, believing the functions listed above to be parts of one single soul.

Referring to the direct understanding of the Torah text, Saadia Gaon shows that the various parts of the soul have their own locations in the human body (*nefesh* in the blood, *ruach* in the heart and *neshama* in the brain). When speaking about the composition of the soul, he states that it is created out of a refined material similar to that of which the heavenly spheres are made.

All of the soul's actions are performed through the body, although Saadia Gaon maintains that cognition can be performed directly by the soul, i.e. without the help of the body. He cites the fact that a person who is blind from birth can see forms in his imagination. We will analyse this view in subsequent chapters, but at this point let us note that modern research is inconsistent with Saadia Gaon's statement. It has now been demonstrated that someone who has been blind from birth does not see images and is not able to perceive light in his imagination.

The main task of the soul is to fulfil the commandments of the Torah. In Saadia Gaon's opinion, by fulfilling the commandments, the soul is filled with light, whereas the soul of a sinner is plunged into darkness.

After death, the souls of the deceased remain beneath the Almighty's Throne of Glory until the moment of the resurrection of the dead. Reward (or punishment) will take place in the World to Come [23].

## 5.3 THE ALTER REBBE'S THEORY OF THE SOUL

The Alter Rebbe begins the outline of his view on the soul with a quote from the book *Tikunei Zohar*: 'The prophet Eliyahu began with the words: "Master of the worlds! When people say that You are One, this word has no numerical significance … You have shown to the world the *tikunim*[59] which we call the ten *sefirot*.'"

Later he writes: 'In its essence, the soul is a whole, indivisible light, which cannot be separated into reason (the *sefirot* of *Chochma*, *Binah* and *Daat*) and *midot* (the six lower *sefirot*). They serve merely as "garments of the soul" – in other words, they belong to the soul but do not relate to its essence.'

The Alter Rebbe notes that reason and *midot* (emotion) present themselves as 'garments', which are not fully separated from the essence of the soul and are connected with it in the same way as the light and vessels in the world of *Atzilut*. At the same time, the Alter Rebbe believes that thought, speech, and action are functions, or the 'garments' of the soul, and are entirely separate from its essence.

The body is also considered to be a 'garment' of the soul, and connected with it in inseparable union. It is important to note that the Alter Rebbe views the interaction between soul and body as a 'two-way street' whereby the soul influences the body and vice versa.

Reason and emotion (the *sefirot* that correspond to these) are viewed as 'tools' used by the soul. At the same time, reason and emotion are subject to change, while the essence of the soul is unchangeable. The Alter Rebbe writes: 'Reason and *midot* [emotions] are nothing other than powers of the soul, which are reflected in the body but do not relate to the essence of the soul.'

Quoting the words of the sages: 'Every blade of grass on earth has *mazal* (a prototype in spiritual worlds), and from *Kohelet*: '…for the Highest over the high waits, and there are higher ones over them' (*Kohelet*, 5:7), the Alter Rebbe emphasises a very important element of Creation, which is that 'Every object or occurrence is influenced from on high during the transition from one level to another, lower one' [9].

In the *Tanya's* opening volume, 'The Book of the Intermediates', the Alter Rebbe makes an interesting remark. He writes: 'In both of them [the body and the soul] there is the same light, and this is present in the same state of inner concealment' [8]. We will analyse this statement in subsequent chapters, but I understand it to be a hypothesis that the soul and the body have identical natures, which are hidden from us.

In reference to the above, it is possible to draw the following interim conclusions.

---

59  Tikunim – adapting, clothing. – *Author's note.*

• The soul is a particular copy of the spiritual worlds, emanating from and created by *Ein Sof*. The soul, like the higher spiritual worlds, contains light and the *sefirot*.

• All the properties of the soul (intellectual, emotional...) are determined by the selection of *sefirot* granted to it as 'garments'.

• All the entities of our world (including the soul) have prototypes (their representations) in the higher spiritual worlds, with which they are inseparably connected; thus, interaction between the prototypes and the entities takes place in two directions (prototype – entity, entity – prototype).

• The soul and the body have the same inner nature, which I assume is information.

While confirming Judaism's traditional division of the soul into five parts (*nefesh, ruach, neshama, chaya* and *yechida*), the Alter Rebbe introduces the concept of the animal, Divine and intellectual souls.

The animal soul is responsible for all the body's vital functions: its desires, feelings and emotions, and for satisfying its material requirements.

As a result of the sin of Adam, good and evil were intertwined, forming the zone of *kelipat nogah*, which forms a kind of intermediary zone between the zone of holiness and the zone of evil. The animal soul is located in *kelipat nogah*, and therefore it can tend towards both good and evil. According to the Alter Rebbe, the source of the animal soul is in the world of *Tohu*, where the 'shattering of the vessels' took place (see Introduction, page 14). The Alter Rebbe writes: 'The source of the animal soul in the higher worlds is higher than the source of the Divine soul, according to the interpretation of the hidden meaning of the words of *Bereishit*: "And these are the kings who reigned in the land of Edom before any king reigned over the children of Israel" (*Bereishit*, 36:31). The king of Israel represents the Divine soul, while the kings of Edom are the animal soul, which is of high origin but fell very low after the shattering of the vessels. Later, it says: "...and he reigned ... and he died"' [9].

The animal soul is clothed in the ten *sefirot*. The intellectual *sefirot* of the animal soul (*Chochma* – wisdom, *Binah* – understanding, *Daat* – knowledge) express the properties of the human reason, which is directed at the material nature of our world. The *midot* of the animal soul (the emotional *sefirot*) represent the evil impulse in the human soul (*yetzer ha-ra*). The Alter Rebbe writes about this, saying: 'The important expression of the animal soul is that it comprehends and knows the material side of this world, its material nature and its crudeness' [10].

The question arises as to why man is given an animal soul. We can find a clue to the answer in the Alter Rebbe's work 'The Book of the Intermediates'. He writes: 'The *Zohar* writes that it is particularly important for a person to sanctify himself at the moment of conjugal union … This is because every *nefesh, ruach* or *neshama* has a garment that proceeds from the essential vitality of his father and the mother' [8].

The Divine soul is the complete opposite of the animal soul. In *Kohelet*, it says: 'God has made one opposite the other' (*Kohelet*, 7:14). The Divine soul is without sin, and all of its strivings are directed towards God. The main task of the Divine soul is to direct the animal soul into the zone of good and towards fulfilling the commandments of the Torah. Its source is the *sefirah* of *Chochma* in the world of *Atzilut*. The Alter Rebbe writes: 'It is known that the soul descends into this world in order to be clothed in a body with a particular aim. Before its descent into this world, it was an integral part of the level of the source of *Atzilut*, where it dwelt in love and awe before the Almighty. But then it descended and was clothed in a body and an animal soul, which conceal and darken the Divine Light. Nevertheless, this descent of the soul is carried out for the sake of its ultimate ascent, since only by descending in this way can the soul acquire the ability to fulfil the will of the Almighty through studying the Torah and observing the commandments.' The Divine soul also possesses ten 'garments' in the form of *sefirot,* whereby the three higher *sefirot* of *Chochma, Binah* and *Daat* constitute the Divine intellect in a person who strives to comprehend the Almighty and the world, while the emotional *sefirot* (*midot*) of the Divine soul represent the good impulse (*yetzer ha-tov*).

There is a constant struggle between the Divine and the animal souls. In 'The Book of the Intermediates', the Alter Rebbe writes: 'Just like two kings fighting for a city where each one wants to conquer it and reign over it, that is, govern its inhabitants in accordance with his will, so that they should submit to his rule in all that he commands them, so, too, do the two souls – the Divine and the animal – battle each other for power over the body and all its limbs. It is the desire and will of the Divine soul to be the body's sole ruler and guide' [8].

As already stated, the task of the Divine soul is to guide the animal soul in the study of the Torah and fulfilling the commandments. The Alter Rebbe stresses that, after a person's death, the soul should return to the higher spiritual worlds clothed in the commandments that it fulfilled in the material world. He writes: 'The commandments serve as garments for the soul in *Gan Eden* [paradise]'. This extremely important view will be analysed below.

## 5.4 THE LOCATION OF THE SOUL

As already noted above, a literal interpretation of the sacred texts leads us to the conclusion that the soul is in the blood, heart and brain. The Alter Rebbe rightly demonstrates that this is not the case. The soul is not an entity of our world, and it does not possess spatial dimensions. In 'The Book of the Intermediates' he states that, in the sphere of the spiritual, the concept of space is inapplicable [8]. The Alter Rebbe also writes that the soul is a simple spiritual entity without any material structure and limitations in terms of space and boundaries, unlike that which is material. The words of the Torah on the location of the soul in the blood or the brain should be understood as a hint towards the point of interaction. There will be a detailed analysis of this in subsequent chapters.

## 5.5 THE SOUL OF THE FIRST HUMAN

The uniqueness of the first human lies in the fact that he was created by the Almighty. All other people have come from people. Consequently, the first human possessed a unique soul. But what was it like? As mentioned above, the animal soul is in the zone of *kelipat nogah*, which was formed as a result of the sin of the first human. This raises the question of the structure of the soul of the first human before the sin. The answer to this can be found in the Alter Rebbe's book *Torah Or*. The Rebbe rightly points out that the creation of the first human differed fundamentally from the creation of plants, animals, birds and fish, whose bodies and souls emerged simultaneously at the command of the Almighty. In the case of the human, the body was created first out of inanimate matter (dust), and only then did the Creator breathe a soul into him. 'And man became a living soul,' it says in *Bereishit*, 2.7. The words 'living soul' appear in the original Hebrew as '*nefesh chaya*'. Therefore, the soul of the first human encompassed all spiritual levels. The inanimate matter corresponds to the *sefirah* of *Malchut*. The Alter Rebbe writes: 'In exactly the same way, in the higher spiritual worlds, *Malchut* is called inanimate nature.' At that point, he introduces an important tenet that the *sefirah* of *Malchut* did not occur by means of the consecutive emanation of *sefirot,* but directly from the higher *sefirah* of *Chochma* [9]. Based on the quotation: 'God founded the earth ['earth' is often a reference to *Malchut*] with wisdom [*Chochma*]' (*Mishlei,* 3:19), as well as an extract from the book of *Sefer Yetzirah*: 'Their beginning is embedded in their end', we can understand that the lower *sefirah* of *Malchut* is directly linked with the higher *sefirah* of *Chochma.*

To reiterate, the level of inanimate nature corresponds to the *sefirah* of *Malchut.* It emanates from the *sefirah* of *Chochma.* On a spiritual level, the *sefirah* of *Malchut* corresponds to the *nefesh* level of the soul, and the *sefirah* of *Chochma,* to *chaya.* Hence it is possible to conclude that the soul of the first human was *le-nefesh chaya* – that is, it encompassed all levels of *sefirot* from the lowest to the highest, with no division between the Divine and the animal soul, and it was located in the zone of holiness and good. As a result of sin, good and evil were mingled, forming the zone of *kelipat nogah* (in between good and evil), and as a result, the soul of the first human, as well as all his descendants, was divided into Divine and animal.

## 5.6 BODY AND SOUL – A SCIENTIFIC APPROACH

In 1995, the Australian philosopher David Chalmers coined the term the 'hard problem of consciousness'. The scholar successfully formulated a problem that had been an object of study and debate for a long time. Chalmers' formula is thus: In what way can the material processes of the brain explain the existence of subjective experience (emotions, thoughts, sensations)?

During the process of studying the interaction between mind and matter, several basic scientific approaches stood out [12].

First of all, let us note that all scientific approaches towards the study of this problem acknowledge the existence of a correlation between mind and the brain. Thanks to the development of neurophysiology, scientists now know which region of the brain is aroused when certain emotions are experienced. It is important to note that, although the causal relationship implies a correlation between cause and effect, the reverse is not always true. The correlation between two systems can take place as a result of their common cause, but not as a result of direct causal interaction.

Let us highlight three of the main scientific approaches to this problem.

1. The materialist approach (reductionism, physicalism).

2. The dualist approach.

3. The theory of indirect interaction.

**1. Physicalism**
The main idea behind this approach is that all mental states and characteristics can be traced back to the fields of matter and physics. This approach states that understanding the workings of the material brain is sufficient in order to understand the workings of consciousness. This approach is not very popular in science today. Physicalism can be refuted by the following arguments:

- It is impossible to explain the existence of '*qualia*' – subjective experience and the quality of the mental state – by describing material processes.

- No physical domain is causally closed, while any solution to fundamental physics equations requires the setting of limits and initial conditions that were not set by the laws of nature.

- The difficulties associated with the concept of 'now' and the present time in the physical description of a system.

The materialist approach implies a direct interaction between mind and matter.

$$\text{MATTER} \longleftrightarrow \text{MIND}$$

**2. The dualist approach**
Supporters of this theory claim that the mind and matter have a fundamentally different nature. These ideas are reflected in the philosophical systems of Plato and René Descartes, who believed that reality consists of physical and mental elements. The main problem with dualism is its inability to explain the interaction between objects that are of a fundamentally different nature.

**3. The theory of indirect interaction**
The supporters of this theory suggest the indirect interaction between reason

and matter through a third, psychophysically neutral category, which can be represented in this way:

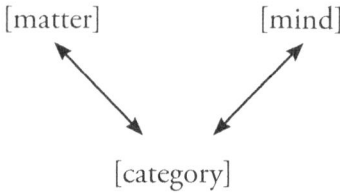

A prerequisite for the theory of indirect interaction is the idea of psycho-physical parallelism, which was developed by Nicolas Malebranche[60] and Gottfried Leibniz.[61] They claimed that the processes occurring in thought and matter corresponded strictly to each other but did not interact at all. Prior to this, though, the medieval philosopher Baruch Spinoza had intro-duced the theory that the mind and matter are based on the same substance and there are diferent modes of it. In the 20th and 21st centuries, the theory of indirect interaction was revisited by scientists working on quantum phys-ics. Among them were Schrödinger, Bohr, Pauli, von Neumann, Penrose, Bohm, and the psychologist Jung. Their main idea was to describe the pro-cesses in neural networks and synapses from the point of view of quantum physics, and to attempt to link quantum physics processes with the theory of indirect interaction.

More and more scientists of that time, including Chalmers, Bohm and others, tended towards the opinion that information is the medium through which reason and material interact. Let us take a closer look at this question.

From David Bohm's[62] point of view, mental and physical processes (states) occurred by dividing the indivisible and psychophysically neutral medium, which the scientist called active information.

---

60  Nicolas Malebranche (1638–1715) – a French philosopher, mathematician, and Cartesian who modified the teaching of Descartes. He expressed the idea that everything that exists in the material world is the idea of God; we recognise things because we recognise God, that is, we contemplate them in God.

61  Gottfried Leibniz (1646–1716) – a German philosopher, logician, mathematician, mechanician, physicist, lawyer, historian, diplomat, inventor and linguist. He was the founder and first president of the Berlin Academy of Sciences, and a foreign member of the French Academy of Sciences.

62  David Bohm (1917–1992) – an American scientist, famous for his work on quantum physics, philosophy and neuropsychology.

Wolfgang Pauli[63] and Carl Jung were very interested in this approach to the problem. Within material reality, they distinguished between ontological (basic) and epistemological (studied) fields. They believed that the same fields also existed in mental reality.

The epistemological field within material reality consists of facts received as a result of the measuring of a quantum system using classical measuring apparatus. The ontological field is the state of entangled systems. These fields are joined together through the process of measurement.

In the mental sphere, the ontological field is represented by the subconscious, and the epistemological field by consciousness. According to Jung's concept, they are joined by the process of the appearance of the conscious mental state from the unconscious, analogous to the process of measurement in the physical dimension. Jung suggested that the field of the subconscious has a collective component that cannot be divided among individuals. This scientist examined the way in which a psychophysical, neutral medium simultaneously covers the 'collective unconscious' and the state of the quantum entanglement of systems. From this field, psychic and physical phenomena are manifest. Some of Jung's ideas resonate with Kabbalah. As mentioned enough, human intelligence is represented by the sefirot Chochma and Bina (sometimes also Daat). According to Kabbalah, the information contained in Chochma cannot be articulated and therefore can be compared to the subconsciousness. Part of it is being formulated in Bina, i.e. at the level of consciousness.

Pauli and Jung called the correlation between the mental and physical fields synchronistic. It is important to note that the third approach represents panpsychism, as well as the existence of mental components in all natural objects.

In the next chapter, we will attempt to show that the theory of indirect interaction, information as a psychophysically neutral medium, and panpsychism can be directly deduced from the ideas of Kabbalah.

---

63  Wolfgang Pauli (1900–1958) – an Austrian-born Swiss theoretical physicist working in the field of elementary particles and quantum mechanics. Laureate of the Nobel Prize in Physics in 1945.

*Chapter 6*

# KABBALAH AS A THEORY OF INFORMATIONAL PROTOTYPES

## 6.1 THE SOUL AND THE BODY

In the previous chapter, I cited the viewpoint of the Alter Rebbe that light is the essence of the soul, and the ten *sefirot* are its garments. Therefore, I see the soul as a complex informational system consisting of light (information about the Almighty) and the *sefirot* (the characteristics given to the soul).

From the text of the Torah on the creation of the first man (dust + soul), we can produce the following definition.

**A person is a complex informational system consisting of two parts. The first part of the system is the the body, coded in DNA, and the second is the soul containing information about the Almighty, determined by the range of *sefirot* attached to it.**

At this point, the reader may justifiably wonder: Why do souls differ from each other, if the ten *sefirot* are always the same?

The reason is that, according to Kabbalah, there are ten main *sefirot* in the system of worlds, and each *sefirah* contains elements of all ten *sefirot*. To use mathematical language, the tree of *sefirot* represents a self-similar structure, i.e. a fractal. Therefore, the number of different combinations of the ten *sefirot* tends towards infinity.

Let us look at an example. The *sefirah Chochma* (wisdom) may be attached to the soul, which is analogous with the main *sefirah* of *Chochma*, or the *sefirah* of *Chochma* that is contained within the *sefirah* of *Chesed*, or the same *sefirah*, but contained within the *sefirah* of *Yesod* from the *sefirah* of *Chesed*, and so on. The set of *sefirot* attached to the soul can conditionally be called its 'DNA'.

From the Torah text about the creation of the first human, it follows that, without a soul, the information system of inanimate matter (dust) does not work according to the principle of DNA coding. Hence it is possible to conclude that the animal soul contains the informational programme for the working of a person's DNA. The properties granted to the animal soul in the form of *sefirot* should correspond to the DNA to a certain extent.

We can draw this conclusion based on the Alter Rebbe's view that a person should sanctify himself before sexual intercourse. It is also evident that a person's characteristics are often similar to those of his parents. When an embryo is formed, the spermatozoon and the egg carry parts of the future DNA as well as parts of the future animal soul. The embryo's animal soul will be analogous to the sum of the parts of the parents' animal soul, although, because both the spermatozoon and the egg can contain different combinations of chromosomes, the child's animal soul will differ as a result from that of its parents.

## 6.2 THE CONCEPT OF DEATH

Based on the views set out above, I propose the following definition of the death of a person.

**Death is the breaking up of a complex information system (a person) into its two components, one of which represents the information system of the 'inanimate matter' (quarks, electrons, etc.), while the other represents the information system that we call the human soul.**

There can be two causes for this collapse, the dysfunction of the body, or the dysfunction of the soul. In the case of the dysfunction of the soul, an example can be found in the Torah.

In the book of Dvorim (Deuteronomy) it is said that Moses, despite his age of 120 was physically healthy. Moses's death was brought about by a 'kiss' of the Almighty, which means that the Almighty interrupted the interaction between Moses's body and soul.

## 6.3 IMMORTALITY OF THE SOUL

Does the concept of death apply directly to the soul?

It is logical to suggest that the death of a soul should be its destruction as an informational system – that is, its information is effectively erased. Within the theory of quantum physics, there is a concept called the '*no delete theorem*', which says that quantum information cannot be destroyed.

Based on this, it seems that an information system can be preserved in its original form, or be divided into separate information systems, but it cannot be destroyed.

## 6.4 INFORMATIONAL PROTOTYPES

Let us remind the reader that, in Chapter 2, we looked at Creation as the development of information systems (worlds) by the Almighty. According to Kabbalah, every entity in a given world, including our world, *Asiyah*, has its roots in the higher worlds. This means that every entity in our world (quark, electron, etc.) has its own informational prototype in all higher worlds.

If we analyse the prophesies of Isaiah and Ezekiel we can conclude the existence of informational prototypes. Isaiah said 'I saw the Lord, sitting on a high and exalted Throne... Seraphim stood around Him' (Isaiah 6:1-2). In the Vision of Ezekiel it is said 'and above the firmament, over their heads, was a likeness of a throne.' According to the Kabbalists as expressed in the commentary of Aryeh Kaplan the prophet Isaiah in his prophecy saw the world of *Beriyah* which contains the Throne of Glory and the Seraphim. The prophet Ezekiel saw the world of *Yetzirah* and the likeness of the Throne of Glory.

To use the language of quantum physics, the interacting entities of our world form an entangled system. Therefore, I believe that a parallel interaction takes place among the informational prototypes in the higher worlds.

If we analyse the prophesies of Isaiah and Ezekiel we can conclude the existence of informational prototypes. Isaiah said 'I saw the Lord, sitting on a high and exalted Throne... Seraphim stood around Him' (Isaiah 6:1-2). In the Vision of Ezekiel it is said 'and above the firmament, over their heads, was the likeness of a throne.' According to the Kabbalists as expressed in the commentary of Aryeh Kaplan, the prophet Isaiah in his prophecy saw the world of *Beriyah* which contains the Throne of Glory and the Seraphim. The prophet Ezekiel saw the world of *Yetzirah* and the likeness of the Throne of Glory.

In relation to the above, all the structures of the human body (DNA, brain, etc.) have their own informational prototypes. At the same time, as shown in previous chapters, the soul cannot be an entity of our world, since it does not have physical dimensions. In *Torah Or*, the Alter Rebbe writes that angels (spiritual entities) can only be manifest in our world in 'special garments' [9]. Let us also recall from the previous chapter the Alter Rebbe's statement that the soul and the body are one and the same light (information).

Concerning the interaction between body and soul, I favour the viewpoint of indirect interaction. Like can only interact with like. I offer the reader the following model. The soul, as an informational system, interacts with the informational prototype of the human body (brain, blood, DNA, and so on). The result of this interaction enters the person's body in our world from its informational prototype. This is a two-way interaction. All the information from our world, which enters a person's body and then enters the person's informational prototype, enters then into the informational system that we call the 'soul'. There it is stored and analysed, and a command is sent back, entering the body of the person via its informational prototype. An essential condition for this interaction is the work of the DNA code in the person's body and, consequently, the circulation of the blood, the work of individual neurons and neural ensembles, etc. However, damage to different parts of the brain alters its informational prototype and accordingly alters the nature of its interaction with the soul. Neurophysiology has long since demonstrated that damage to different parts of the brain leads to the destruction of many functions (memory loss, inability to feel, changes in the person's emotional state, etc.). According to Kabbalah, the *sefirot* are attached to the soul in a certain potential state, and they are capable of growing – that is, their informational capacity and ability to analyse can increase. This process occurs as a result of the soul receiving information through the body's informational prototype (teaching the soul). Thus, the level of actualisation of the *sefirot* correlates to the person's intellectual behaviour in our world.

However, the soul does not only interact with the informational prototype, but also participates in other informational processes. In Chapter 2 we talked about how Creation is constantly being renewed by the Almighty, how it is a dynamic informational process with 'two-way traffic', and how the human being is an important element in this. Hence the soul, and in particular its intellectual part, expressed by the *sefirot* of *Chochma*, *Binah* and *Daat*, participates in the two-way information process with the higher spiritual worlds and with other souls.

It should be noted, though, that the level of the soul's participation in this depends on its appeal to God, and this is where a person's Divine soul comes in. As an informational system, the soul can receive information not only through the body but also from the higher *sefirot*. Only by actively developing the intellect and appealing to God can a person achieve the heights of understanding the structure of our world. It is no coincidence that the great scientists such as Newton, Maxwell, Einstein and so on, who changed our perception of reality, believed in God.

As can be seen from the above, the theory of the indirect interaction between body and soul has been expressed by many scientists (Bohr, Pauli, Jung et al.), and a similar theory can be derived from Kabbalah. The 'collective unconscious', as proposed by Jung, could be the result of the interactions of a certain part of the soul with the souls of others. It should be noted that the souls of all people and the informational prototypes of their bodies exist in a single informational space, and they are more or less connected with each other. We will analyse this theory below.

## 6.5 MEASURING ROD, SOUL, BODY AND CYBERNETICS

The concept of the measuring rod is extremely important in Kabbalah. It is found in the highest *sefirah, Keter,* and is the root of *Chochma* (wisdom). Let's recall that everything is created by 'His Wisdom'. My understanding of the measuring rod is that everything in the worlds, including our material world, is measured, finite and proportionate to the state of total perfection. In His great wisdom, the Almighty gave every created entity a precise amount of informational life force, so that each entity could fulfil its assigned mission. There are trillions of electrons in our universe, but they are each identical to the other; the same goes for protons, neutrons, etc. This fact has puzzled and surprised many scientists of the 20th and 21st centuries. In my opinion, this is one of the phenomena that confirm that everything was created with the measuring rod.

It is my position that, no matter what, no combination or action with or to protons, electrons etc. can qualitatively change the informational exchange within creation, i.e. it cannot give rise to life. For life to arise, this combination must be connected with a qualitatively different informational system, the soul, which is contructed in the image of the higher spiritual worlds.

As already mentioned in previous chapters, according to Kabbalah, during the process of Creation, a 'shattering of vessels' occurred in the world of *Tohu,* and the zone of *sitra achra* (the side of evil) was formed, where information about the 'self' significantly exceeded information about the Almighty. *Sitra achra* consists of *kelipot* (husks) containing sparks of light (information about the Almighty). According to Arizal's view, the main task of the soul is to implement correction (*tikun*) through the process of *birur* – raising sparks of Divine Light (information) from the *kelipot* to their source, thereby achieving the destruction of evil. The only way in which the soul can do this is by studying the Torah and fulfilling the commandments. As already noted above, not being an entity of this world, the soul cannot fulfil the commandments on it own, as the commandments can only be fulfilled in the material world. It is for this purpose that the soul was given the body, and thus was the 'human' entity formed.

At this point, a comparison emerges with cybernetics, as described in the works of Norbert Wiener[64] and William Ashby.[65] The main concept in cybernetics is that a person invents mechanisms and builds machines that are capable of increasing and developing his abilities. For example, a hammer increases a person's muscular strength and a computer increases the intellectual capacity of his brain. In his work, Ashby rightly pointed out that there is no clear boundary between a person and a machine, or between a person and his environment. A person influences the machine and the machine influences the person. Meanwhile, a person's body is like an environment for the brain. This way, we can consider a new entity: a man-machine system.

In the same way, the Almighty created the body in order to increase and perpetuate the ability of the soul to fulfil the commandments in the material world, having created an entity – man (body + soul).

## 6.6 GARMENTS OF THE SOUL

In the previous chapter, we introduced the theory of the Alter Rebbe from 'The Book of the Intermediates' that the commandments serve as garments for the soul in the higher worlds. The Alter Rebbe often introduces his theories in the form of hints. Let us attempt to analyse this in more detail.

In the process of fulfilling the commandments and studying the Torah and natural sciences, a transition takes place for the *sefirot* of the soul from a potential state to an actual one. Their informational capacity is increased, along with the ability to analyse, and the level of the soul's participation in the two-way process of exchanging information with the Almighty becomes greater. As a result, the soul is able to accept more light (information). After a person's death, the soul's ability to learn and fulfil the commandments ceases.

In the higher worlds, with the 'drawing closer to the source', the quantity of perceived information grows. Hence, the greater the soul's informational

---

64  Norbert Wiener (1894–1964) – an American scientist, eminent mathematician, philosopher and founder of cybernetics and the theory of artificial intelligence.

65  William Ashby (1903–1972) – an English psychiatrist and cybernetics specialist who carried out pioneering research into complex systems.

capacity, the closer to the source (the Almighty) it will be in the higher worlds. This is what lies behind the Alter Rebbe's equations of the commandments with the 'garments' of the soul.

## 6.7 ON THE QUESTION OF HELL (*GEHENNA*)

As already mentioned, the Jewish position on hell (*Gehenna*) is brief and altogether vague. There is no one single opinion. Without claiming to be right, I offer my view on this question.

As noted above, the main task of a person's Divine soul is to correct his animal soul. This task can be:

• Carried out in full.

• Partially carried out.

• Not carried out at all.

In the first case, this is a completely righteous person whose Divine and animal souls will end up in *Gan Eden* (paradise), with the individuality they acquired during life still intact, and participating fully in the two-way information process. This is mentioned in the *Talmud* thus: 'The righteous will delight in the reflection of the light of the *Shekhinah* in *Gan Eden*.' (The *Shekhinah* is the Divine presence and corresponds to the *sefirah* of *Malchut*.)

In the second case, the soul contains information about violation of the commandments (evil), which must be removed from the soul's informational system, and this takes place in *Gehenna* (allegorically with the help of fire or snow).

I do not rule out that, in the third case (the complete sinner), the whole of the soul's information system consists of evil, and after processing in *Gehenna,* not a single part of the informational system will remain to be presented in *Gan Eden* and participate in the process of the resurrection of the dead. Such a soul will have no share in the World to Come.

According to the Alter Rebbe's view, evil is also present in the higher spiritual worlds. However, although good was mingled with evil in our world as a result of the sin of Adam, in the higher worlds good and evil are separate. Therefore, the soul, in which good and evil are mingled as a result of sin, cannot exist in that way in the higher worlds, so it must pass through *Gehenna* [9].

*Chapter 7*

# MENTAL SPACE

A person's mental space can be conditionally described using a vector in a multidimensional space. Let us take a closer look at this.

It is evident that this space contains the dimensions of the person's emotional state, connected with *midot* (the *sefirot* of *Chesed, Gevurah, Tiferet, Netzach, Hod* and *Yesod*); dimensions connected with intellect, memory, understanding and knowledge (the *sefirot* of *Chochma, Binah* and *Daat*); and the dimensions of will and desire (the *sefirah* of *Keter*).

Therefore, a person's state at a particular moment in time can be represented by a vector in a multidimensional mental space where the starting point shows the person's state at a given moment, while the vector shows the direction of movement in the mental space. The mental space also contains images of people, things and events with which the person has been connected at some time. There is a passive mental connection with these images. At the moment when we think about one of these images, the mental space changes from passive to active. The more time we think about an image, the more powerful the mental connection becomes. A particular neural ensemble in the person's brain corresponds to each powerful mental connection. In Chapter 2, I explained the view that evil caused by a person corresponds to a severing of positive mental connections. Accordingly, neural ensembles cease to receive energy, which is expressed in the person's physical suffering.

People's mental spaces are subspaces of spiritual worlds and are connected with each other with various forms of correlation. People who are able to sense subtle correlations are usually called psychics or clairvoyants.

This raises the question that has always been asked by humanity: How and where should we move in our mental space?

The answer is not obvious. One of the main concepts of Kabbalah is the theory of *tikun* (the process of correction), during the course of which evil will be destroyed and the world will become better; this is the main aim of a person's life. In order to accomplish this task, a person should constantly activate the most important mental connection – the connection with God.

Note that here I do not refer to mystical connections, which are practised in prophetic Kabbalah by means of extended fasting, meditation, and singing hymns. By establishing a simple mental connection with God, a person can change his life, since his every movement in mental space, which is henceforth expressed in practical actions, will become directed towards achieving God's purpose.

In this way, a person's mental space can be divided into different areas:

• Acceptance of God and His laws.

• Non-acceptance of God and His laws.

• The area in between.

Let us attempt to describe this division from a scientific point of view.

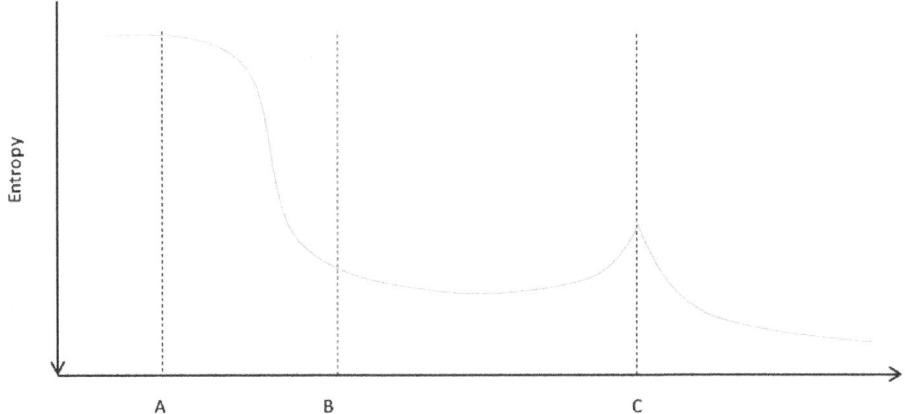

Fig. 7. Mental phase space

The most stable state in phase space is a state with maximum entropy. Therefore, the greater the number of combinations in which we can repeat this state, the more stable it is. In my opinion, evil is a high entropy state, while good is low entropy. For a person to change his inner state to 'good', a lot of spiritual work is required. In Fig. 7 we can see the transitional zone (B to C), which corresponds to the state of ordinary people, who don't do a lot of good, but nor do they do a lot of evil. To the left of the transitional zone, the zone of good begins (A to B). This is the zone of people who the Alter Rebbe calls the 'intermediates'. These people have fully suppressed evil within them, but have not destroyed it. The intermediates have to continue their spiritual work, because if they stop, evil will return, as it is not destroyed. To the left of point A is the zone of righteousness. The righteous have fully destroyed evil and therefore their spiritual work is complete and there is no chance of evil returning.

At point C, a person loses the connection with the *sefirot* of the Divine soul, and joins with the *sefirot* of the side of evil (*sitra achra*), then falls into a zone whose entropy is higher than that of the intermediate state.

Unlike the *sefirot* of the Divine soul, the opposite *sefirot* take a person's energy, giving practically nothing in return. Returning from this zone to the intermediate zone or the good zone is extremely difficult. To do this, a person must bring judgement upon himself, having entered into a connection with the *sefirah* of *Gevurah*, establish a connection with the Almighty, and cease doing evil. Having done this, a person has the opportunity to return and even become righteous.

On this subject, it says in the Talmud that a repentant sinner is more precious to the Almighty than a righteous person. This is because of the huge mental work that a person must do in order to return from the zone of evil.

The above system can be described in the terms of quantum computing. Let's imagine the *sefirah* of the animal soul. It has two connections: 1) to the *sefirah* of the Divine soul and 2) to the *sefirah* of evil (*sitra achra*). These two connections can be viewed as a binary quantum system – a Qubit. In the case of the fully righteous, the connection to the Divine soul takes on a value of 1 and the connection to *sitra achra* takes on a value of 0. For an absolute sinner, the values are reversed, and there is an infinite number of intermediate points.

*Chapter 8*

# KABBALAH AND PHILOSOPHY

I believe that the traditional distinction between the philosophical and mystical (Kabbalah) orientations in Judaism is inaccurate. Both of them have the same direct attitude towards philosophy. While the main Jewish philosophers such as Saadia Gaon, Maimonides and Hasdai Crescas[66] adopted some principles of Aristotle's philosophical stance, Kabbalah coincides to a certain extent with the philosophy of Plato, and to a larger extent with the philosophy of Neoplatonism, which is inherent in the idea of Divine emanations and the hierarchical structure of existence.

At the beginning of the 20th century, as a result of turbulent developments in science, in particular quantum physics and the theory of relativity, a new trend emerged in philosophy – process philosophy, founded by the brilliant English mathematician Alfred North Whitehead (1861–1947). However, the roots of this trend can be found in the philosophy of antiquity, which can be divided into two movements: statistical (substantive) and dynamic. The most prominent representative of the former was the philosopher Parmenides, who stated that behind all visible phenomena there is a single, unmoving reality. The originator of the 'dynamic movement' was Heraclitus of Ephesus, who uttered the well-known words '*Panta rhei*' ('Everything flows'). Heraclitus is rightly considered the founder of process

---

66  Rabbi Hasdai Crescas (1340–1411) – a philosopher, theologian, statesman and head of the Spanish Jews in the 14th century. He was the Rabbi of Saragossa. He is considered one of the original Jewish philosophers, and of the Middle Ages in general. Crescas's innovative views on eternity and nature, and space and time, facilitated a move away from Aristotelianism towards natural philosophy, as a result of which it became possible to create a new form of physics – classical mechanics.

philosophy. The idea of process philosophy was later developed by Plotinus with his Neoplatonic philosophy, Gottfried Leibniz and Hegel, and was developed more fully in the works of Alfred Whitehead.

In my opinion, the main concepts behind process philosophy have much in common with – and are sometimes even exactly the same as – the ideas of Kabbalah. In Whitehead's philosophy, the world is represented as a network of interacting processes. This is its fundamental concept. Whitehead rejects the statistical model of reality. Every object is constructed through its own interactions, and exists only as a result of interactions with a system and each of its elements. In turn, every event that occurs then influences others. According to Whitehead, the basic unit of reality is the entities called 'actual occasions', which are based on information and have mental and material poles. Each 'actual occasion' grows out of all the information available in the universe [24]. Whitehead sees the world as a highly integrated dynamic structure of interacting events, which has been built on a hierarchical basis (atom – molecule – cell – organ – organism). According to Kabbalah, Creation (the world) represents a dynamic structure in which the process of deploying and exchanging information does not cease for a single moment, thus all its entities are interconnected and exercise influence on each other.

Whitehead's philosophy rejects the dividing of the world into its physical and mental components. According to process philosophy, the problem of the interaction between mind and body disappears if we accept the processes of transferring information, whereby mental and physical aspects are manifest in various circumstances, as the basic components of reality.

This concept coincides completely with the theory of the aligning of informational prototypes during the interaction between the body and soul, as examined in earlier chapters, and which emanates from Kabbalah.

The supporters of process philosophy believe it is not only the Almighty who can create, but also man, to a certain extent, given that man was created in the likeness of the Almighty.

Another of the main theories of Kabbalah is the large role and authority given to man over Creation. As already mentioned in previous chapters, Creation cannot function without mankind's participation in the information process. According to Kabbalah, mankind was given authority and the task of completing Creation through the process of correction (*tikun*) and the destruction of evil.

The views of process philosophy are similar to those of panpsychism, believing that everything in nature has its own mental component. This theory directly coincides with Arizal's concept.

In his own philosophy, Alfred Whitehead acknowledges two characteristics of the Almighty: 'consequent nature' and 'primordial nature' [27]. 'Primordial nature' is God's knowledge of all possible worlds in their potential form, while 'consequent nature' is understanding the essence of all the active processes in the world.

Here we can see an analogy between the concepts of the higher knowledge of *Ein Sof* and the lower knowledge in the system of *sefirot*, as introduced by the Alter Rebbe and examined in previous chapters.

In describing the relationship between God and the world, process philosophy adopts a position of panentheism. Panentheism is the intermediary position between pantheism and classical theism. In pantheism, the world is identical to God, whereas in classical theism the world is an outer manifestation of God. In panentheism, God is transcended and immanent in the world.

This view completely coincides with Kabbalah, which occupies a standpoint of panentheism.

Theistic process philosophy believes that all seemingly coincidental changes and processes in the world are aimed at fulfilling God's ultimate aim, which completely coincides with Kabbalist views.

Therefore, we can see that Kabbalist ideas on the dynamic and never-ceasing nature of Creation, on the huge role of man therein, on the relationship between God and the world, on information, are confirmed by the ideas that humanity has acquired as a result of the rapid development of science in the 20th century.

*Chapter 9*

# ARE THERE INFINITIES IN OUR WORLD?

In his book *What We Cannot Know*, Marcus du Sautoy, professor of mathematics at the University of Oxford, asks: 'Are there things that science will never be able to know?'

In this same book, he gives an interesting definition of an atheist. In du Sautoy's opinion, an atheist thinks that we can know everything, while a believer considers our knowledge to be limited [15].

In this chapter, I will try to answer the question: Are there infinities in our world? – referring to both infinitely large and infinitely small quantities.

## INFINITY

The main scientific method consists of finding mathematical connections between phenomena A and B, and extrapolating from this. As far as explanations are concerned, there are two variants: either science does not know why phenomenon A occurred, or it explains that phenomenon A occurred as a consequence of phenomenon C. However, phenomenon C also requires an explanation. In this case, we have infinite regression, although if we prove that infinite regression does not exist in our world, then by following the chain of cause and effect, we will arrive at the cause of all causes, i.e. God.

In *The Guide for the Perplexed*, Maimonides postulated the absence of infinite magnitudes in our real world. He wrote: 'There is no infinite magnitude, and there is no infinite quantity of finite magnitudes.' The same view was shared by Saadia Gaon.

In *Torah Or,* the Alter Rebbe writes about the concept of 'the measuring rod' (*botzina deqardinuta*), which is the root of the *sefirah* of *Chochma* in the world of *Atzilut.* Referring to a verse from *Tehillim*: 'You have made them all with wisdom' (*Tehillim,* 104:24) and the words of Yeshayahu: 'Who has measured the waters in the hollow of his hand?' (*Yeshayahu*, 40:12), he suggests that everything in our world is measured by the Almighty, and therefore it is finite [10].

Galileo Galilei wrote: 'The difficulties in the study of the infinite arise because we attempt, with our finite minds, to discuss the infinite, assigning to it those properties that we give to the finite and limited; but this is wrong, for we cannot speak of infinite quantities as being the one greater or less than or equal to another.' The great German mathematician Carl Friedrich Gauss wrote: 'I protest above all against the use of an infinite quantity as a completed one, which in mathematics is never allowed.'

Thinkers from Aristotle to Newton to Gauss considered only 'potential' infinities. Things changed in the 19th century when George Cantor developed set theory, and introduced the notion of countable and uncountable infinities.

In the article 'The Infinity Illusion' (written by the American science writer Amanda Gefter in the special issue of *New Scientist*, Infinity and Beyond), it is said:

'For physicists, however, the infinite paradise has become more like purgatory. To take one example, the standard model of particle physics was long beset by pathological infinities, for instance in quantum electrodynamics, the quantum theory of the electromagnetic force. It initially showed the mass and charge of an electron to be infinite.

'Decades of work, rewarded by many a Nobel prize, banished these nonsensical infinities – or most of them. Gravity has notoriously resisted unification with the other forces of nature within the standard model, seemingly immune to physicists' best tricks for neutralising infinity's effects. In extreme circumstances such as in a black hole's belly, Einstein's equations of general relativity, which describe gravity's workings, break down as matter becomes infinitely dense and hot, and space-time infinitely warped.'

**It is particularly important to understand the difference between purely abstract mathematics and our real world.** For example, whatever number we may think of, we can always add one, and the resulting number will be larger. However, in reality, the largest number we can record is limited by the quantity of particles in the universe. Someone might say that it is not necessary to record the number as it can be invented, but in this case the highest number we can invent is limited, either by the length of our lives or by the computer's resources.

About two and a half thousand years ago, Zeno, a pupil of the philosopher Parmenides, proposed his famous paradoxes: 'The dichotomy', 'Achilles and the tortoise' and 'The arrow' (an interested reader can find plenty of information about these on the Internet), which, to this day, still have no clear explanation.

The essence of Zeno's paradoxes was that someone wanting to pass along a distance from zero to one must first reach the halfway point, then half of halfway, and so on ad infinitum – that is, the person must carry out an infinite number of operations in finite time. With this, Zeno proved that movement can never be completed, and it cannot even begin. It is very important to understand that, when solving Zeno's paradoxes, a distinction must be made between the purely mathematical abstractions and real space and time.

Zeno's ideas divided the scholars of ancient Greece into atomists and supporters of the continuum [12]. This division continues to this day. Aristotle was a supporter of the continuum, while Democritus and Leucippus were atomists. The supporters of the continuum claimed that between any two points that are infinitely close to each other, there is always a minimum of one more point. The atomists stated the principle of discreteness – that is, the existence of a minimum indivisible segment.

The supporters of discreteness argued that, as a result of infinite division, immeasurable points are formed, from which it is impossible to add up to a whole. The supporters of the continuum, in particular John Dan Scott, put forward a theory that accepting discreteness means destroying Pythagoras' theorem.

The great scientist and thinker Nicolas of Cusa stated that, in an ideal situation (abstract) infinite divisions exist, but the real world is discrete, so there are minimal indivisible magnitudes in space and time. However, in the 16th century, at the beginning of the scientific revolution, scientists were in need of practical mathematical instruments for physical calculations. In connection with this, Johannes Kepler[67] introduced the concept of infinitesimal quantities in order to calculate the movement of the planets. The concept of

---

67  Johannes Kepler (1571–1630) – a German mathematician, astronomer, mechanician, optician, and pioneer of the laws of planetary motion in the solar system.

infinitesimal quantities was perfected by Cavalieri, a pupil of Galileo. René Descartes[68] used them in his calculations. Later, Newton and Leibniz developed differential calculus based on the concept of infinitesimal quantities. This approach is called mathematical atomism.

On its own, the concept of infinitesimal quantities was rather ambiguous. On one hand, it was infinitesimal, but on the other it was still a quantity. Moreover, the ratio of two infinitesimal quantities (the derivative) is a perfectly real number. It is important to note that infinitesimal quantities are still used in physics calculations today.

From a philosophical point of view, infinitesimal quantities were a compromise between the continuum and discreteness.

In the 19th century, the mathematicians Augustin-Louis Cauchy[69], Richard Dedekind[70] and Karl Weierstrass[71] began to work on infinitesimal quantities. Cauchy introduced the concept of limits. Thus, it was considered that by introducing the concept of limits, to which the sum of an infinite quantity of infinite numbers tends, a solution is found to Zeno's paradox. Once again, though, it is important to differentiate between a mathematically abstract solution and a solution in space and time. Not all mathematicians accepted the methods of Cauchy. The following example illustrates the complexity of working with infinity (Cauchy).

Let us note the following infinite sequence: $1 - 1 + 1 - 1 + \ldots$

It can be written down in two ways:

1. $(1 - 1) + (1 - 1) + \ldots$ in this case, the result of the infinite sequence is zero.

2. $1 + (1 - 1) + (1 - 1) + \ldots$ in this case, the sequence is equal to one.

---

68   René Descartes (1596–1650) – a French philosopher, mathematician, mechanician, physicist and physiologist who founded analytical geometry and modern algebra, as well as the method of radical doubt in philosophy and mechanical philosophy in physics.

69   Augustin-Louis Cauchy (1789–1857) – a French mathematician and mechanician, member of the Paris Academy of Sciences, the London Royal Society, the St Petersburg Academy of Sciences, and others. He developed the foundations of mathematical analysis, and made a huge contribution to analysis, mathematical physics and many other fields of mathematics. He was one of the founders of continuum mechanics. His name is among those of the great French scientists listed on the first floor of the Eiffel Tower.

70   Richard Dedekind (1831–1916) – a German mathematician, known for his work on abstract algebra and the definition of real numbers.

71   Karl Weierstrass (1815–1897) – a German mathematician and 'father of modern analysis'.

Cantor rejected the need for infinitesimal quantities in mathematics. However, in the 20th century, a new mathematical viewpoint called 'non-standard analysis' emerged, which restored the use of infinitesimal quantities. In the 20th century, Zeno's paradoxes were reformulated to create 'supertasks' [22]. The concept of a supertask was formulated by the logician James Thomson. The question posed was as follows: Is it possible to complete a supertask, i.e. to complete an infinite number of operations in finite time? It is quite obvious that if completing the final step is considered to be the completion of the supertask, then the supertask cannot be completed. Thus, we arrive at atomism. However, one question remains: What should we do about Pythagoras?

In the 20th century, a new mathematical theory – 'discrete geometry' – began to develop. Its main tenet was discreteness. Since discrete geometry moved away from pure mathematical abstract, it was accepted that real points have dimensions, and real lines have width. The scope for discussion here is very wide but, to be brief, it can be said that, although it is not altogether unambiguous, discrete geometry was used to prove that Pythagoras' theorem was not invalid.

However, let us return to physics for a moment. In the 17th century, the great scientist Leibniz proposed his famous hypothesis that 'nature does not make a jump'. Modern science refutes this.

Scientists in the 19th century were puzzled by the paradox of black-body radiation. According to continuous wave theory, a black body should radiate an infinite quantity of energy, but that is absurd. A solution was found by the young German physicist Max Planck, who demonstrated that if discreteness is assumed (quantum radiation), theoretical calculations will agree fully with experiments. In 1905, Albert Einstein explained the photoelectric effect, using the principle of discreteness (quantisation), for which he was awarded a Nobel prize.

In modern theories of quantum gravity, it is assumed that space and time are discrete and the notion of indivisible parts of space and time (chronons) has been introduced.

After discussing the infinitely small, let us now discuss the infinitely large. In mathematics, a point where a function tends to infinity is called a singularity. In the real physical world, scientists differentiate between open and closed singularities. No one has ever observed open singularities (i.e. the application of a force of infinite magnitude). The majority of scientists believe that open singularities do not exist in our real world, since the application of a force of infinite magnitude would lead to absolute chaos in space and time. Science considers the moment of the Big Bang to be a closed singularity, as well as the singularity in the centre of a black hole. Let us conditionally call them 'points of creation'.

When a body (a star) collapses under the effect of its own gravitation to within its Schwarzschild radius, light loses its ability to leave the space of the collapsed body, and nothing can prevent its further collapse to the point of a singularity (infinite density) [14]. (The Schwarzschild radius for our sun is equal to approximately 3 kilometres/1.9 miles, and for planet Earth it is less than one centimetre/⅓ inch.) The point of no return in the space of a black hole is called an event horizon.

This conclusion concerning the existence of a singularity in a black hole comes from the solving of Albert Einstein's equation of the theory of general relativity. However, there is one problem.

Modern science is having difficulty giving a precise definition of the concept of a singularity. From a mathematical point of view, a singularity is the collapse of space and time, which raises the question: What is at the point of a singularity?

Attempts have been made to describe a singularity as a point on a 'unfinished path' (meaning that the path of any particle that has fallen into the singularity is interrupted), the concept of missing points in space and time, and the pathology of the curvature of space and time. However, all of these descriptions are vague and incomplete.

In the majority of modern scientific theories, it is considered that the conclusion that a singularity exists at the centre of a black hole, or at the moment of the Big Bang, shows that, in this case, the theory of general relativity is being applied beyond the boundaries of its application, and therefore it is wrong to conclude that a singularity is present.

From the same article by Amanda Gefter, mentioned above, it is said:

'But it is at the Big Bang that infinity wreaks the most havoc. According to the theory of cosmic inflation, the universe underwent a burst of rapid expansion in its first fraction of a second. Inflation explains the features of the universe, including the existence of stars and galaxies. But it cannot be stopped. It continues inflating other bits of space-time long after our universe has settled down, creating an infinite "multiverse" in an eternal stream of big bangs. In an infinite multiverse, everything that can happen will happen an infinite number of times. Such cosmology predicts everything – which is to say, nothing.

'This disaster is known as the measure problem, because most cosmologists believe it will be fixed with the right "probability measure" that would tell us how likely we are to end up in a particular sort of universe and so restore our predictive powers. Others think there is something more fundamental amiss. "Inflation is saying, hey, there's something totally screwed up with what we're doing," says cosmologist Max Tegmark of the Massachusetts Institute of Technology (MIT). "There's something very basic we've assumed that's just wrong."

'For Tegmark, that something is infinity. Physicists treat space-time as an infinitely stretchable mathematical continuum; like the line of real numbers, it has no gaps. Abandon that assumption and the whole cosmic story changes. Inflation will stretch space-time only until it snaps. Inflation is then forced to end, leaving a large, but finite, multiverse. "All of our problems with inflation and the measure problem come immediately from our assumptions of the infinite," says Tegmark. "It's the ultimate untested assumption."'

In the string theory exists a Holographic Principle, which states that the description of the volume of space is encoded on a low dimensional boundary to the region. Using the Holographic Principle, Jabob Bekenstein came to the conclusion that black holes are maximum entropy objects and that they have more entropy than anything else of the same volume. He introduced the so-called Bekenstein Bound, which is the upper limit to the density of information in a certain volume. As the amount of information is related to the total degrees of freedom of matter (energy), Bekenstein inferred that the matter in a certain volume could not be subdivided infinitely many times. There must be a level of fundamental particles.

Based on the above, I come to the conclusion that modern science confirms the ideas of Jewish thinkers and the Kabbalistic concept of the measuring rod, i.e. that our world is finite.

So, can we know everything?

In answer to this question, I suggest we recall the incompleteness theorem of the great Austrian-born mathematician Kurt Gödel (1906–78), who said that within any system of consistent axioms there are statements that are true, but unprovable from within the system.

My personal view (without claiming to be correct) is as follows:

**There is a limit to our knowledge, and we cannot know everything, but we should follow the path of the process of acquiring knowledge as if there were no limits.**

*Chapter 10*

# THE TORAH AND MATHEMATICS

When approaching the Torah from a scientific point of view, we should be very careful, remembering the words of the seventh Lubavitcher Rebbe, who said that the Torah is an absolute truth, while science is relative. The Torah is not a physics textbook. Except on rare occasions when the Torah speaks openly in the language of figures, we should not seek scientific formulae in the Torah. Rather, the Torah contains the basic ideas concerning our world order, upon which scientific formulae are based.

In the 19th and 20th centuries, a series of brilliant theoretical predictions were made ('with the point of a pen') concerning the existence of natural phenomena, which were subsequently confirmed by experiments. Thus, in 1846, while analysing the orbit of Uranus, Urbain Le Verrier[72] calculated the position of the as yet undiscovered planet Neptune. In 1915, Albert Einstein predicted the existence of gravitational waves in the universe, which was confirmed in 2016. In 1928, the English physicist Paul Dirac predicted the existence of the anti-electron (positron), which was proven by means of experimentation in 1932. In the 1960s, Peter Higgs[73] et al. predicted the existence of the Higgs boson, which is responsible for giving mass to all

---

72   Urbain Le Verrier (1811–1877) – a French mathematician specialising in celestial mechanics, who spent most of his life working in the Paris observatory. His most famous achievement was predicting the existence of the planet Neptune, which he did through the mathematical analysis of astronomical observations.

73   Peter Higgs (born 1929, England) – a British theoretical physicist and currently emeritus professor at the University of Edinburgh. He was awarded the Nobel Prize in Physics in 2013.

elementary particles. Fifty years later, the Higgs boson was discovered as a result of experiments in the Large Hadron Collider.

In my opinion, all the above facts are direct proof that the law given to our world by the Almighty during Creation is written in the language of mathematics. Galileo Galilei was speaking about this when he stated, 'The laws of nature are written in the language of mathematics.' Mathematical laws are universal and not time-sensitive. Numbers are the basis of mathematics. Zero and one are given a special place among them all.

The fundamental concepts of Judaism are the Oneness of the Almighty and the creation of the world out of nothing – *ex nihilo*. In mathematical terms, these concepts correspond to one and zero. It is hard to overestimate the significance of the concept of Absolute Nothing. Zero is the most difficult number to understand in mathematics. Our intellect is not capable of grasping the essence of Absolute Nothing. There is no equivalent of Absolute Nothing in our universe. Even if we look at the concept of a vacuum, we should understand that it exists in space and time and has a residual energy level, known as a vacuum energy, and therefore Absolute Nothing does not exist.

The concept of the world's creation *ex nihilo* can be found in the sacred texts. It was first mentioned in the book of our forefather Abraham, *Sefer Yetzirah*, where it is written: 'And He created that which exists out of that which does not exist.'

The concept of *ex nihilo* was later developed in the works of Saadia Gaon (*The Book of Beliefs and Opinions*), Maimonides (*The Guide for the Perplexed*) and the founders of Hasidism.

I would like to emphasise that 'nothing' is a unique concept and is completely beyond our comprehension. We cannot ask 'what is nothing?' or 'where is nothing?'.

Without zero as a separate number, and therefore without negative and complex numbers, mathematics cannot function. Zero did exist in Egyptian and Babylonian numerical systems as a kind of place holder, but not as a number in its own right. The ancient Greeks, and in particular the followers of Pythagoras, who put forward a theory that our world is made of numbers, began their numbers with the monad – the number one. They did not include zero as a separate number. They posed the question: 'How can *something* appear out of nothing?' We will answer this question shortly.

The concept of zero as a separate number, as well as that of negative numbers, was introduced by the Indian mathematician and astronomer

Brahmagupta in the seventh century AD.

In the 19th century, set theory was developed. In set theory, zero is denoted as an empty set, a set that contains nothing. I would like to note that the idea that 'something' (a set) contains 'nothing' is already mind-bending. The empy set is unique in many ways. For example, the empty set is a subset of all sets; at the same time, there is no set that is a subset of the empty set. In number theory, 1 is denoted as the set that contains the empty set, 2 is denoted as the empty set, and the set containing the empty set and so on for all the other numbers. Thus we can see that all numbers are made up of empty sets, and we can say that numbers, the language of nature, are made up entirely of 'nothing'.

However, let us return to the ancient Greeks' question. How can something come out of nothing? We know from mathematics that the figure zero can exist on its own, or it can occur as a result of combining positive and negative numbers. For example, $-5 + 5 = 0$. Today, many eminent physicists share the idea that the sum of the energy in our universe is equal to zero. This means that the positive energy of mass is exactly balanced with gravity's negative potential energy. This theory was first proposed by Edward Tryon[74] in 1973. Its view is shared by authoritative scientists such as the American theoretical physicist Alan Guth, founder of the theory of cosmic inflation, and Stephen Hawking, who wrote: 'This negative gravitational energy exactly cancels the positive energy represented by the matter.' Guth, meanwhile, noted: 'In particular, the energy of a gravitational field is negative. This statement, that the energy of a gravitational field is negative, is true both in the context of the Newtonian theory of gravity and also in the more sophisticated context of Einstein's theory of general relativity.' And this is the answer to the question posed by the Pythagoreans.

The Torah sometimes openly talks in the language of numbers and this pertains to the story of Noah's Ark.

When reading the Torah, we are guided by the principle that it does not contain a single superfluous letter. Every letter and even punctuation mark has meaning. The Almighty clearly showed Noah the geometric measurements of the ark: 'And this [is the size] you shall make it: three hundred cubits the length of the ark, fifty cubits its breadth, and thirty cubits its height. You shall make a skylight for the ark, and to a cubit you shall finish it to the top.' Here is a geometric illustration of God's words:

---

74  Edward Tryon (born 1940) – an American scientist and professor of physics.

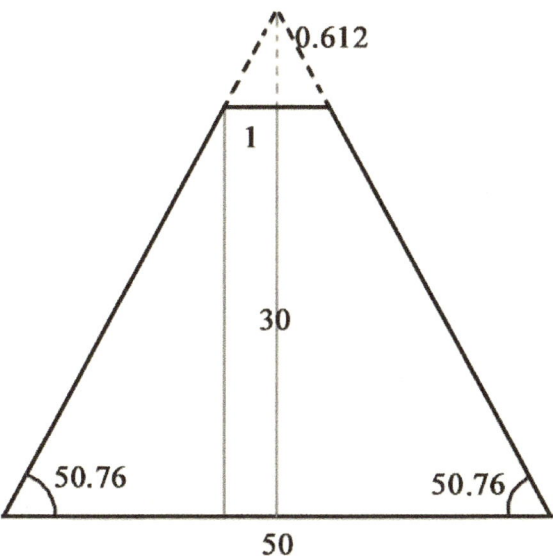

Fig. 8. The geometry of the ark

From Fig. 8 we can see that the ark was in the form of a truncated pyramid. The angle of inclination on the side of the ark is equal to 50.76°. The angle of inclination of the Pyramid of Cheops is equal to 51.52°. The angle of inclination of the Pyramid of Khafre is equal to 52.2°. The angle of inclination of the Pyramid of Menkaure is 50.47°. Therefore, it is clear that the angle of inclination on the side of the ark corresponds to the angles of inclination of the three pyramids of Giza, allowing for a margin of error.

Based on the above, we can make a bold supposition that **the Egyptian pyramids were built in the form of Noah's ark**.

If we take the ratio of the sum of the width and height of the ark to its width:

(50 + 30.612) / 50, we get 1.612. The ratio of the ark's width to its height is 50/30 ≈ 1.667. The same ratio for the Pyramid of Cheops is approximately 1.631. The value of the **golden ratio** φ is approximately 1.618. The number φ is a universal irrational number, like π. In this situation, the slight deviation from φ in the ark's ratios is explained by the fact that the Almighty gave the measurements to Noah in whole numbers.

The golden ratio is defined as the point whereby a section is divided off at a proportion of approximately 68/32. Euclid was the first to study the golden ratio in mathematics, in 300 BC. He showed it to be present

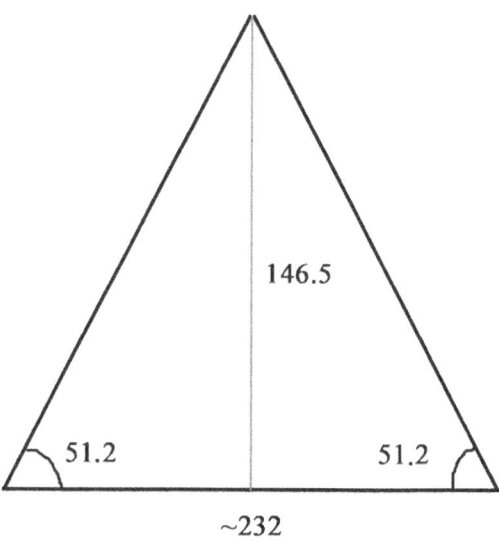

Fig. 9. The geometry of the Pyramid of Cheops

in different geometrical figures. The golden ratio was studied by medieval mathematicians and is still being studied by mathematicians today. These include Leonardo of Pisa (Fibonacci), the astronomer Johannes Kepler, and Roger Penrose. Fibonacci, the great 12th-century mathematician who introduced algebra to Europe, created the sequence that bears his name. In the Fibonacci sequence, each number is the sum of the previous two numbers (i.e.1, 1, 2, 3, 5 etc.); the further up the sequence we go, the closer the ratio of the last number to its predecessor gets to φ. The golden ratio is often encountered in art, music, architecture, nature (in the structure of leaves, and the parts of the human body), the structure of galaxies, and also at an atomic level.

Once again, this example shows us that the Torah contains the fundamental mathematical principles by which our world was made.

*Chapter 11*

# CONCLUSION

## THE QUANTUM WORLD TO COME

In the Woody Allen film *Café Society*, a Jewish gangster converts to Christianity before his execution, giving the explanation that there is no life after death in Judaism. Many Jewish believers can often be heard expressing the same view. This is a huge error. A fundamental principle of the Jewish faith is the belief in the life of the soul after death, in the coming of the Mashiach, in the resurrection of the dead, and in the advent of the World to Come.

However, despite the firmness of these views, the details by which they are described – e.g., the time at which they take place, the forms in which the body and soul will exist, etc. – are expressed in complex terms, sometimes even ambiguously, so that the subject has been, and still is, the subject of serious debate in Judaism. In this chapter, I would like to analyse the opinions of Jewish religious authorities on these events from the point of view of modern scientific knowledge.

We will not find any direct references to the resurrection of the dead, the coming of the Mashiach, or the advent of the World to Come in the text of the Torah proper (i.e., the Five Books of Moses). Maimonides and Saadia Gaon explain this by saying that, when He gave us the Torah, the Almighty, in His wisdom, wanted to direct us towards fulfilling the commandments in this world, and consequently to receive reward and punishment in this world, without distracting our attention with distant subsequent events. Any explicit information about the resurrection of the dead was communicated later, in the prophecies. The Almighty said to Yechezkel: 'Say to them, Lo! I open your graves and cause you to come up out of your graves as My people'

(*Yechezkel*, 37:12). The prophet Yeshayahu declared: 'May Your dead live, corpses shall rise' (*Yeshayahu*, 26:19). In the book of the prophet Daniel, it says: 'And many of those who sleep in the dust of the earth shall awake, some to everlasting life, and some to shame and everlasting contempt' (*Daniel*, 12:2). On this subject, *Kohelet* says: 'And the dust returns to the earth as it was, and the spirit returns to God, Who gave it' (*Kohelet*, 12:7). Similarly, we can find information about the coming of the Mashiach and the World to Come in the prophecies.

THE VIEWPOINT OF MAIMONIDES

Maimonides expresses the following views on the World to Come:

• Unlike the animal part of the soul, the intellectual part is not subject to destruction.

• Our world has a beginning, but it has no end.

• The resurrection of the dead will take place with the coming of the Mashiach. However, death will not disappear, and people will continue to die.

• The World to Come already exists in parallel to our world, and we will dwell in it in spiritual form.

Maimonides wrote: 'The soul of any flesh is its idea, granted to it by God.' This is referring to intellect, which is the idea of the soul. The animal part of the soul, which gives life to the body and exists only with it, will disappear upon the body's demise. But the idea will not disappear, since its actions are not dependent on the life-giving soul. On the subject of the coming of the Mashiach, Maimonides wrote: 'Do not imagine that, in the days of the Mashiach, the laws of nature will be abrogated or that something new will appear in the world. Nothing of the sort will happen – the laws of the world will not change.' Maimonides believed that, in accordance with the prophecies, at the time of the coming of the Mashiach the Jewish people will gather in the land of Israel where the Third Temple will be built. Concerning the resurrection of the dead, Maimonides suggested that it may take place shortly before the coming of the Mashiach, simultaneously as the Mashiach is arriving, or immediately afterwards. On the subject of the World to Come,

Maimonides wrote: 'We suppose that the present reality will be preserved forever, and nothing in it will change, apart from a few details – this would be a miracle.' In his opinion, the resurrection of the dead is not the ultimate goal. The ultimate goal is the World to Come, regarding which he says: 'In the World to Come there will be no bodies, as our teachers told us, and there will be no food or drink and no sexual relations.'

Maimonides also emphasised that: 'Everything that is separate from the material exists in greater reality than that which possesses matter; there is nothing more real, since separate existence is true (actual) existence as it is not subject to change' [7].

Maimonides did not discuss the question of the reincarnation of souls (*gilgul*) and the punishment of souls in hell (*Gehenna*).

## THE VIEWPOINT OF SAADIA GAON

Saadia Gaon believed that, after death, a person's soul will be beneath the Divine Throne of Glory until the time when the number of souls allotted by the Almighty is reached. After that the Mashiach will come, and the resurrection of the dead will take place. The main difference between the views of Saadia Gaon and Maimonides is as follows. Citing the words of the prophet Yeshayahu: 'For behold, I create new heavens and a new earth' (*Yeshayahu*, 65:17), Saadia Gaon states that, shortly after the coming of the Mashiach, our world will be destroyed, and a new reality will occur – the World to Come, in which we will exist in our bodies. Saadia Gaon pays much attention to the question of what life will be like in the World to Come. Commenting on the writings of the sages: 'There will not be eating and drinking in the World to Come', Saadia Gaon states that bodies will be sustained by light.

When speaking about punishment, Saadia Gaon briefly mentions *Gehenna*, referring to the book of the prophet Yehoshua (Joshua), although he does not explain what *Gehenna* is like, and what kind of punishment will be there. He categorically denies the possibility of reincarnation (*gilgul*) [23].

As an example of the possibility of existing without food and drink, Maimonides and Saadia Gaon refer to Moses' forty-day sojourn on Mount Sinai. This example is very important, and we will return to it later.

## THE VIEW OF KABBALAH

According to this concept, after a person's death, part of the soul (the *nefesh*) remains in the grave and undergoes the 'punishment of the grave' for its sins. The part of the soul called *ruach* is also punished for its sins, but after 12 months it ascends to the lower *Gan Eden*. The part of the soul called *neshama* returns to its origin and ascends to the upper *Gan Eden*, where it remains until the moment of the resurrection of the dead. The soul returns to the upper *Gan Eden* clothed in the commandments and the good deeds it has accomplished in our world, and it exists in the world of souls until the resurrection of the dead. The reincarnation of souls or parts of souls may occur (generally as a punishment for forbidden sexual relations). The souls of the righteous can be subject to reincarnation for the purpose of supporting the world. The concept of *Gehenna* is particularly vague and viewed as a kind of spiritual purification. According to the *Zohar*, the soul of the Mashiach dwells in a special place in *Gan Eden*, called the 'Bird's Nest'. In our material world, the Mashiach will first appear in Upper Galilee. The kingdom of the Mashiach will be accompanied by wonders, the flickering and falling of stars, and so on. At the time of the Mashiach, redemption will mean a return to the perfection that was destroyed by the sin of Adam. Divine revelation will increase in the world. The mysteries of the Torah will be opened up. The Messianic era will continue for around a thousand years. The resurrection of the dead will occur at the end of the era of redemption on the great Day of Judgement [2].

According to Nachmanides, after a normal physical life, resurrected bodies will be purified and find themselves in the future spiritual world that will come after the destruction of our world. In that world, we will exist in the form of souls clothed in spiritual bodies, and preserve our own individuality. Some Kabbalists, including Hasidic Masters, believed that, in the World to Come, souls will be clothed in real bodies. According to Kabbalah, Mashiach will come when the process of correction (*tikun*) is complete – that is, when all the sparks of holiness return from the zone of *kelipot* and into the zone of holiness, and evil disappears from our world.

## THE SOUL AND THE MATERIAL BODY

In order to analyse the above opinions and concepts, let us attempt to define the soul and the material body. As we discussed earlier in the book (see

Introduction, page 10), according to *Sefer Yetzirah*, the Almighty created all the worlds with the twenty-two letters of the Hebrew alphabet and the ten *sefirot*, which are called numbers. Both letters and numbers are an informational code. (This concept is similar to the ideas of the Pythagoreans, who claimed that our world is made up of numbers – i.e., an informational code). Moreover, there is no difference in this regard between the creation of the spiritual and the creation of the material world. The difference lies only in which letters are used: the spiritual worlds were created with the letter *yod* of God's name, whereas the material world was created with the letter *hei* from the Divine name. Hence it is possible to conclude that information is the basis of all reality, both spiritual and material. Modern science is also gradually coming to this conclusion. The information in quantum systems cannot be destroyed. All the processes of the transformation of energy and matter are based on informational exchanges.

The fact that both the spiritual and material reality are made up of information is a form of the philosophy of monism, and will help to solve an important Kabbalist question: 'If everything that exists is God, and our material world has many forms, then God must change, and this contradicts the concept of the unchangeability of the Almighty' (in the words of the prophet Malachi, 'For I, God, have not changed' (*Malachi*, 3:6)). Given the theory that information is the single basis of reality, we can answer this question.

According to the teaching of Arizal, the spiritual worlds – *Atzilut* (the world of emanation), *Beriah* (the world of creation), *Yetzirah* (the world of formation) and our material world *Asiyah* (the world of action) – contain the tree of the ten *sefirot*. In Kabbalah, the concept of *sefirot* is described as a vessel that possesses a particular property (for example, *Chochma* – wisdom, *Binah* – understanding, and so on), and is filled with light. In addition, all the *sefirot* are connected with each other, and each of them contains the ten other *sefirot*. In fact, the world of the *sefirot* has the structure of a fractal and tends towards an infinite number of combinations of the ten *sefirot*.

From a scientific point of view, we understand that the concept of *sefirot* in the form of a vessel filled with light is an allegory, as neither space, nor vessels, nor light (as we understand them) exist in the spiritual worlds. From my point of view, the *sefirah* is an informational system in which two forms of information are contained and interact. Light is information about the existence of the Almighty and His essence. The vessel is information about one of the 'attributes' or traits of the Almighty, as expressed in the system of *sefirot*. *Chesed* is expansion, love, and kindness. *Gevurah* is contraction, strictness, and judgement. Let us clarify this with an example. When we say: 'This person is good', we are not only giving information about his character, but also about the fact that he exists.

However, let us now return to the concept of the soul. In *Torah Or*, the Alter Rebbe gives this definition: 'The soul is essentially an integral, indivisible light which cannot be separated into intellect and *midot*.' (*Midot* are the six lower *sefirot*, and 'intellect' is the three higher *sefirot: Chochma* (wisdom), *Binah* (understanding) and *Daat* (knowledge).) The intellect and the *midot* serve only as the 'garments of the soul' – in other words, although they belong to the soul, they do not relate to its essence. Hence, we can conclude that the soul is constructed according to the principle of the tree of *sefirot*. Its essence is light – that is, information about the existence of the Almighty; while the ten *sefirot*, or the garments of the soul, are information about the soul's properties. Since, as mentioned above, there are a great many combinations of *sefirot* in the spiritual worlds, then there are also a great many souls, possessing varying combinations of characteristics. The likeness of the soul to the tree of *sefirot* is indicated by a verse from the first chapter of the book of *Bereishit* (Genesis) about the creation of man 'in the image and likeness' of God (*Bereishit,* 1:26).

The ten *sefirot* (the ten properties of the soul) can be likened to a person's DNA.

In the language of quantum physics, a person's soul is non-local and non-separable. Let us decode this concept. Systems are called local if their properties are defined by their location in space and time. Systems are called separable if their properties are determined only by the inner qualities. A person's soul possesses the property of 'vertical' non-separability, since it is connected with its root in the higher spiritual worlds, from whence it came, as well as possessing the property of 'horizontal' non-separability. The person's body affects his soul, and also the souls of other people. We will explain this in more detail shortly.

In quantum mechanics, the state of any system is reflected in a multidimensional Hilbert space where every point corresponds to a particular state of a quantum system. In the same way, the state of our soul can be described using the concept of 'multidimensional mental space'. Our consciousness has a large number of different states and combinations thereof, and can be described at a given moment by a particular point in the multidimensional mental space. There could be intersections of the mental spaces of different people. In particular, if two people were to think about each other, even though they were separated in space, they would exist at the same point in multidimensional mental space. Here is another example: according to the viewpoint of Judaism, at the moment when the Torah was presented at the foot of Mount Sinai, the souls of all Jews were present, including all who had lived in the past and all who were destined to be born. Thus, all Jews without exception were united in multidimensional mental space at the point of the Sinai revelation.

In contrast to the soul, the material objects of the classical world are quasi-local and quasi-separable. 'Quasi' because, although quantum correlations do exist, they are extremely small. Why macroscopic objects lose their quantum properties is one of the main questions in quantum physics. One explanation is the process of decoherence – informational exchange with the environment. As a result of this exchange, the system loses its quantum properties and acquires 'classical' ones. Correspondingly, there is also a reverse process called recoherence, meaning that when a system is fully isolated from the environment, it can lose its 'classical' properties and transition to a state of superposition (a different reality). At the present time, experiments are being carried out to show that, where the informational exchange is absent, relatively large objects can manifest quantum properties (carbon molecules, i.e. buckyballs, aluminium oscillators).

Let us return to Moses' sojourn on Mount Sinai. The Alter Rebbe writes: "'And Moses went into the midst of the cloud, and he went up the mountain, and Moses was upon the mountain for forty days and forty nights" (*Shemot*, 24:18). Moses did not eat or drink during this time, and his material body was fed with spiritual food, like an angel. Here the cloud that surrounded Moses is significant … It also served as food for Moses' [9]. The Alter Rebbe also writes that the angels can only enter our world in special garments, and people can only go up to the world of the angels in special garments. What does the Alter Rebbe mean here? We know from physics that the material body cannot survive for forty days without water, and, consequently, without the reverse process (excretion). However, Moses was covered by a cloud. In my opinion, the cloud isolated Moses from the exchange of information with the environment. As a result, recoherence took place, and Moses' body took on an intermediate form (non-material), which did not need and could not perceive material sustenance.

The second example concerns the first man and woman, Adam and Eve. Let us note a few important points. Adam and Eve were in a special place, the Garden of Eden, and according to Kabbalah, one of the consequences of Adam's sin was the 'increased level of the material nature of our world'. Before the sin, Adam had not given his wife a personal name, but just called her 'woman' (*isha*). From this, it is possible to conclude that, before the sin, Adam and Eve in *Gan Eden* were not in the fully material state to which we are accustomed. The essence of the sin was the reading of forbidden information about good and evil, which corresponds to the physical understanding of decoherence. As a result of this, the bodies of Adam and Eve acquired classical properties (in the words of *Bereishit* (Genesis) 3:21, 'God made for the man and his wife garments of skin'). Adam became aware that before him there was a separate being, and he gave his wife the name Hava (Eve). In their classical material state, the first man and the first woman could no longer be immortal and dwell in *Gan Eden*, so they were banished from it.

Let us also note that the level of decoherence in the various spiritual worlds is not the same. Since in the world of *Atzilut* (emanation) there is only light and the *sefirot*, the vessels are therefore one with the light, i.e. there is practically no decoherence. In the world of *Beriah* (creation), the vessels are no longer one with the light and so separate informational entities appear (*Gan Eden*, souls and archangels), i.e. decoherence is manifested. Decoherence is further intensified in the world of *Yetzirah* (formation), where countless numbers of angels dwell. Finally, decoherence reaches its maximum in the world of *Asiyah* (our material world) where we perceive material substance in the form of distinct objects.

From all of the above, I draw the following conclusion. The World to Come will not be material in our classical understanding of the concept. Like the spiritual worlds, it will be a world of partial recoherence, where our bodies and souls will be joined as one. However, we cannot talk about the classical material nature of our bodies. We do not know what the level of recoherence will be. In my opinion, the Kabbalists have come closest to the correct answer, as they have said that the prototype of the World to Come has been given to us in the Torah in Moses' sojourn on Mount Sinai, and that of Adam and Eve in *Gan Eden*.

# BIBLIOGRAPHY

1. Doronin, S. *Kvantovaya magiya* [Quantum magic]. M., Physika, 2007.

2. *Zohar*. M., Eksmo, 2013.

3. Idel, M. *Kabbalah. Novye Perspektivy* [Kabbalah. New Perspectives] M., Gesharim–Mosty Kultury, 2010.

4. Nechipurenko, V. N. *Yevreiskaya filosofiya I kabbalah. Sefer Yetzirah. 32 Puty Mudrosti. Obyasnenye desyati sefirot Rabbi Azriel is Gerony* [Jewish Philosophy and Kabbalah. *Sefer Yetzirah*. 32 ways of Wisdom. Rabbi Azriel of Gerona's explanation of the ten *sefirot*] (new Russian translation from ancient Hebrew). Rostov on Don, Yu.F.U., 2007.

5. Penrose, R. *The Emperor's New Mind* (Russian version). M., Editorial URSS, 2003.

6. Rabbi Judah Halevi. *Sefer ha-Kuzari*. M., Knizhniki, 2014.

7. Rabbi Moses ben Maimon (Maimonides). *Putevoditel Rasteryannykh* [The Guide for the Perplexed]. Jerusalem–Moscow, Gerashim–Mosty Kultury, 2010.

8. Rabbi Shneur Zalman of Liadi. *Tanya*. M., FEOR, 2005.

9. Rabbi Shneur Zalman of Liadi. *Torah Or*, Vol.1. M., Knizhniki, 2013.

10. Rabbi Shneur Zalman of Liadi. *Torah Or*, Vol.2. M., Knizhniki, 2016.

11. Atmanspacher, Harald. 'Quantum Approaches to Consciousness.' *Stanford Encyclopedia of Philosophy* (Summer 2015 Edition), Edward N. Zalta (ed.), URL = <https://plato.stanford.edu/archives/sum2015/entries/qt-consciousness/>.

12. Bell, John L. 'Continuity and Infinitesimals.' *Stanford Encyclopedia of Philosophy* (Summer 2017 Edition), Edward N. Zalta (ed.), URL = <https://plato.stanford.edu/archives/sum2017/entries/continuity/>.

13. Bub, Jeffrey. 'Quantum Entanglement and Information.' *Stanford Encyclopedia of Philosophy* (Spring 2017 Edition), Edward N. Zalta (ed.), URL = <https://plato.stanford.edu/archives/spr2017/entries/qt-entangle/>.

14. Curiel, Erik and Bokulich, Peter. 'Singularities and Black Holes.' *Stanford Encyclopedia of Philosophy* (Summer 2018 Edition), Edward N. Zalta (ed.), URL = <https://plato.stanford.edu/archives/sum2018/entries/spacetime-singularities/>.

15. Du Sautoy, Marcus. *What We Cannot Know*. London, 4th Estate, 2016.

16. Faye, Jan. 'Copenhagen Interpretation of Quantum Mechanics.' *Stanford

*Encyclopedia of Philosophy* (Fall 2014 Edition), Edward N. Zalta (ed.), URL = <https://plato.stanford.edu/archives/fall2014/entries/qm-copenhagen/>.

17. Floridi, Luciano. 'Semantic conception of information.' *Stanford Encyclopedia of Philosophy* (Spring 2017 Edition), Edward N. Zalta (ed.), URL = <https://plato.stanford.edu/archives/spr2017/entries/information-semantic/>.

18. Hafner, Katie and Lyon, Matthew. *Where Wizards Stay Up Late: The origins of the internet.* New York, Simon & Schuster, 1996.

19. Healey, Richard. 'Quantum-Bayesian and Pragmatist Views of Quantum Theory.' *Stanford Encyclopedia of Philosophy* (Spring 2017 Edition), Edward N. Zalta (ed.), URL = <https://plato.stanford.edu/archives/spr2017/entries/quantum-bayesian/>.

20. Jacobs, Louis. *Seeker of Unity: The life and works of Aaron of Starosselje.* London, Vallentine Mitchell, 2006.

21. Lorenz, Hendrik. 'Ancient Theories of Soul.' *Stanford Encyclopedia of Philosophy* (Summer 2009 Edition), Edward N. Zalta (ed.), URL = <https://plato.stanford.edu/archives/sum2009/entries/ancient-soul/>.

22. Manchak, John and Roberts, Bryan W. 'Supertasks.' *Stanford Encyclopedia of Philosophy* (Winter 2016 Edition), Edward N. Zalta (ed.), URL = <https://plato.stanford.edu/archives/win2016/entries/spacetime-supertasks/>.

23. Saadia Gaon. *The Book of Beliefs and Opinions.* Yale University Press, 1976.

24. Seibt, Johanna. 'Process Philosophy.' *Stanford Encyclopedia of Philosophy* (Winter 2018 Edition), Edward N. Zalta (ed.), URL = <https://plato.stanford.edu/archives/win2018/entries/process-philosophy/>.

25. Scholem, Gershom. *Kabbalah.* New York, Penguin Books, 1978.

26. Vaidman, Lev. 'Many-Worlds Interpretation of Quantum Mechanics.' *Stanford Encyclopedia of Philosophy* (Fall 2018 Edition), Edward N. Zalta (ed.), URL = <https://plato.stanford.edu/archives/fall2018/entries/qm-manyworlds/>.

27. Viney, Donald. 'Process Theism.' *Stanford Encyclopedia of Philosophy* (Summer 2018 Edition), Edward N. Zalta (ed.), URL = <https://plato.stanford.edu/archives/sum2018/entries/process-theism/>.

# LIST OF ILLUSTRATIONS